Beautiful America's

Northwest Victorians

Front Cover: Marshall House, Fort Vancouver, 1886

Published by
Beautiful America Publishing Company
P.O. Box 244
Woodburn, Oregon 97071

Design: Ancel Van Renes

Library of Congress Catalog Number 2001035647

ISBN 0-89802-727-6
ISBN 0-89802-726-8 (Paperback)

Printed in Korea

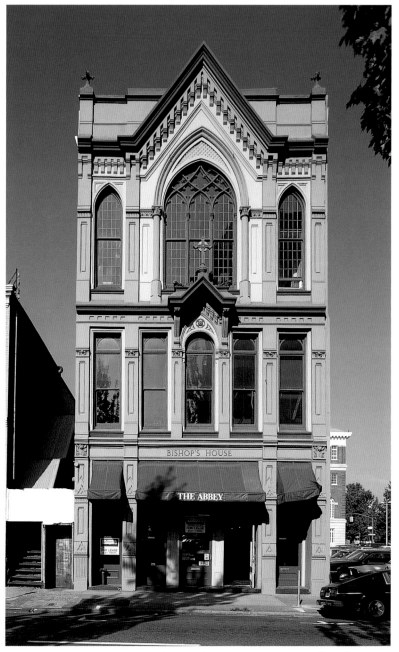

The Bishop's House, Portland, 1879

Beautiful America's

Northwest Victorians

Text & Photography
by
Kenneth Naversen

Contents

Introduction

The Picturesque Frontier

In the Pacific Northwest, as in the rest of the United States, nineteenth-century builders relied heavily on books and periodicals for practical, aesthetic, even moral advice on architecture. In the early Victorian period the works of Andrew Jackson Downing, author, editor, landscape gardener, were particularly influential. A persistent ideal in his writings, "tasteful simplicity," is exemplified in a house that is still standing today on a bluff overlooking the Columbia River.

Built in 1857, the *Fort Dalles Surgeon's Quarters (p. 6)* was based on a design for "A Symmetrical Bracketed Cottage" featured in *Downing's Architecture of Country Houses (1850)*. As the author noted, the basic plan is enhanced by some simple but effective details: hooded and bracketed windows; vertical board-and-batten siding; a projecting gable over a small porch, and an entry way surmounted by a Gothic arch. Commenting on these features, Downing wrote:

No person would build such a quaint yet modest porch as this, no one would give this simple character of beauty to the windows, and no one would reach this exact height of tasteful simplicity in the whole exterior character, unless he had a real appreciation of the beautiful and truthful in cottage life...

This was not mere aesthetics. For Downing "the beautiful and truthful" made architecture a powerful tool in the struggle for civilization.

So long as men are forced to dwell in log huts and follow a hunter's life, we must not be surprised at lynch law and the use of the bowie knife. But when smiling lawns and tasteful cottages begin to embellish a country, we know that order and culture are established.

Perhaps Captain Thomas Jordan, the officer in charge of construction at Fort Dalles, and Louis Scholl, the German draftsman who adapted the plan from Downing's book, had these civilizing thoughts in mind when they built this "tasteful cottage" at this outpost on the Oregon frontier. Or maybe they just wanted to add a touch of style to what was then the most important fort on the upper Columbia. Whatever the reasons, they availed themselves of several other plans featured in Downing's book when they were charged with the task of enlarging the fort in the late 1850s. Among their creations were three roomy and stylish cottages that were to serve as quarters for the commanding officer and his subalterns. Under Jordan and Scholl's direction, a similarly styled house was also constructed for the commanding officer at Fort Simcoe, which lay seventy miles to the north in the recently established Washington Territory.

When the buildings were completed, the officer and his chief assistant had reason to be pleased. The work had been finished expeditiously and–given the price of labor on the frontier–at a reasonable cost. Moreover, the buildings they had created were handsome and well built. Jordan was confident that they would serve Fort Dalles for many years to come. What is more, the occupants of the new houses, especially the ladies, lost little time in expressing their satisfaction with the appearance and layouts of their new quarters.

But if the officers and wives of Forts Dalles and Simcoe were pleased, higher-ups in the chain of command were not. It was not long before Jordan and Scholl received official criticism for their efforts. A colonel who had seen the new buildings at Fort Dalles opined in a report that they were "entirely unsuited to a Military post on the frontier." And soon after the commander of the army's Pacific division inspected the fort, he issued a pointed decree that all future military construction in the area was to be of the "plainest kind." The Army, it seems, had little appreciation for "the beautiful and truthful in cottage life."

Though Jordan and Scholl failed to win the approval of their superiors, they succeeded in leaving the Pacific Northwest with two extraordinary architectural landmarks, one in Oregon, the other in Washington. The *Surgeon's Quarters* at Fort Dalles and the *Commanding Officer's Quarters* at Fort Simcoe *(pp. 6-7)* are the only remnants of this unique experiment in romantic military

Fort Dalles Surgeon's Quarters, The Dalles, 1856

Commanding Officer's Quarters, Fort Simcoe, c.1857

architecture—the "Picturesque Frontier" described in Priscilla Knuth's admirable monograph of the same name. The other buildings Scholl adapted from Downing's designs have long since succumbed to fire and other perils.

That these extraordinary houses were built at all is indicative of the region's early willingness to embrace new architectural styles. That two of them have survived to the present, is indicative of its commitment to maintaining concrete expressions of its own history.

As the photographs in this book should serve to demonstrate, Oregon and Washington have managed to preserve many other architectural treasures from the late nineteenth century. We can only hope that this will continue to be the case far into the future—that among other architectural landmarks, the Downingesque cottages that Scholl and Jordan built nearly a hundred and fifty years ago will still be standing when the next century dawns.

Northwest Victorians

Although their respective inhabitants can be relied upon to concoct, assert, and insist upon various alleged differences between them, the sovereign states of Oregon and Washington have much in common. Besides a mutual border and a coterminous location in the northwest corner of the lower forty eight states, the two have similar climates and geographies and spectacular, rim-side seats on the eastern shore of the vast Pacific. Their origins are also similar. They were explored and settled at about the same time and by the same people. Indeed, they once belonged to the same political entity, the original Oregon Territory. Moreover, as the examples of Fort Dalles and Fort Simcoe suggest, the two states share a common architectural heritage.

Settlement of the region that was to become Oregon and Washington began in earnest in the early 1840s and was complete in all essentials by the turn of the century. By that time rail links to the east had been established, and the two territories had both achieved statehood. Meanwhile, the pioneers had performed the monumental task of carving a working society out of the wilderness—building roads, establishing farms, founding cities, and erecting buildings by the thousands. Since this sixty-year period of settlement and early development coincided exactly with the reign of Queen Victoria, it should come as no surprise that much of the region's early architecture bears the stamp of that era.

But what exactly is Victorian architecture? From the point of view of style, it was a decidedly mixed bag. It ranged from the quaint Gothic Revival of Downing's day to the flamboyant Queen Anne that held sway at the end of the century. It included modish imports such as the refined Italianate and haughty French Second Empire as well as such home-spun building modes as the Stick and Shingle styles.

But for all this diversity, Victorian buildings, especially the houses, shared certain qualities that distinguished them from their predecessors and their successors. For one thing, they generally loved ornament. In the late nineteenth century even modest homes were partial to decoration, and the bolder ones were florid in the extreme. The exact form of decoration varied from decade to decade and style to style, but the tendency to make use of it was a constant throughout the era. Carved bargeboards and flat-cut gingerbread marked the Gothic Revival; elaborate lintels and eaves brackets, the Italianate; lathe-turned spindlework and patterned shingles, the Queen Anne.

Another characteristic of Victoriana was a proclivity to sprout fanciful extensions of all sorts. Towers, turrets, rambling wings, bay windows, wraparound porches, gazebos, cupolas, belvederes, pinnacles, and high-flying chimney stacks were some of the means by which the houses of the era achieved picturesque form…and, in the process, broke free of the boxy shapes that had imprisoned their ancestors.

Yet another ingredient in the mix was a sense of drama, a certain spirit of make believe and "let's pretend." Victorian houses were like actors trying on costumes from long ago and far away. By donning the appropriate architectural trappings, they sought to evoke not only the appearance but also the spirit of the romantic past and the exotic present.

This sense of theater was a reflection of the profound romanticism of the nineteenth century. And it is this, more than anything else, that separates the architecture of the period from that of the classical and the modern eras. It explains why Victorian houses often resembled Medieval castles, French chateaux, Gothic cottages, Persian villas, and a host of other models, some real, some merely fanciful. Often, in fact, they found inspiration in sources that were as much literary as architectural—hence all those castellated parapets, nooks, crannies, and tower hideaways right out of Sir Walter Scott.

The concept of the "picturesque" was another important component of the Victorian world view. In architecture this manifested itself as the conviction that a building should harmonize with its natural surroundings. The picturesque movement, which began as a reaction to classicism, had its roots in England. There, in the late eighteenth century, landscape designers took to placing picturesque "ruins" at strategic locations on the estates of their wealthy patrons. The idea was to enhance the pictorial qualities of the grounds. It was only a matter of time before the main houses also took on the character of stage sets, as in the case of Horace Walpole's Gothic-inspired *Strawberry Hill*. Before long, artistically placed and romantically configured dwellings had became the height of fashion.

When it arrived in America a few decades later, the picturesque was quickly embraced by architects and landscapers. It is no accident that Andrew Jackson Downing, who played such an important role in promoting the new movement in the United States, was the son of a landscape gardener. His influence, which was greatest in the Northeast, was felt across the entire country, even, as we have seen, in the remote regions of the Pacific Northwest. His conviction that "irregular" compositions in the Gothic or English Cottage modes were especially appropriate for the rough-hewn American wilderness, led directly to the novel experiments in military architecture essayed by Thomas Jordan and Louis Scholl.

Greek Survivals

Although the picturesque Gothic and Italianate styles dominated early domestic architecture in Oregon and Washington, survivals from earlier periods also made an appearance. The *McLoughlin* (1846) and *Ainsworth* (1855) houses, for example, represent modes that had already gone out of fashion in the east by the time they were built in Oregon City. The former, which belonged to the chief agent of the Hudson's Bay Company, was a large, framed box in the Georgian style. The latter, which is probably the best example of a Greek Revival style house in the Pacific Northwest, was built in imitation of a prostyle temple with four columns surmounted by a broad entablature and triangular pediment. Other good regional examples of the Greek Revival include the *Bybee-Howell House* on Sauvie Island, the *Rothschild House* in Port Townsend and the *Orr House* in Steilacoom.

The Greek Revival is not usually included in the Victorian canon, but perhaps it should be, at least in its latter years. It has been excluded because it was, by definition, "classical," and Victoriana is generally seen as a romantic reaction to classicism. But if the *forms* of the Greek Revival were classical, its allusive impulses were, at heart, romantic. By representing the trappings of ancient Greece, these houses were asserting symbolic connections between the historical democracy of Athens and the new republic that had sprouted on the American continent. As Mary Mix Foley has pointed out, the Greek Revival was an important model for the romantic revival styles that followed on its heels. It showed that buildings could be important for their associations as well as their utilitarian functions. This notion of architecture as stage set, of course, was an aspect of the picturesque movement.

Some simple Greek Revival houses indicate their allegiance with the barest of references—fluted corner boards suggesting classical piers or columns; side and transom lights around the front door; broad cornices reminiscent of a full classical order. With its entry and gable end turned toward the street, even a basic clapboard house could be made to suggest something of the Greek Revival. This front-gable plan can be seen in the *Crosby House* in Tumwater *(p. 10)*, a dwelling which also has some Gothic Revival fetters— steep gables and wavy vergeboard most notably.

The Gothic Revival

The Gothic Revival, one of the styles championed by A. J. Downing, flourished in the east from the 1840s until the Civil War. But in the Pacific Northwest it had an even longer life. Decades after the style had gone out of fashion, it continued to exert a persistent influence on Victorian house building in the region. It was also the

Robert Newell House, Newberg vicinity, 1852

Milne House, Oregon City, 1869

Crosby House, Tumwater, c.1858

Fellows House, Oregon City, 1867

A.V. Peters House, Eugene, c.1870

11

dominant style for church architecture.

As with the Greek Revival, Gothic Revival houses often showed their leanings with the barest of references. A central gable prominently placed on the front of a side-gabled clapboard box was a common means of adding a touch of Gothic styling. One of the earliest houses in the Northwest to follow this formula is the *Newell House* near Newberg *(p. 10)*. It was built in 1852 by a mountain man who guided one of the first wagon trains to the Willamette Valley, and, except for its centered gable, it might have been just another vernacular pioneer home. More elaborate examples of the same basic idea can be seen in the *Fellows* and *Milne* houses in Oregon City *(p. 10)* and the *Libbey House* in Coupeville *(p. 14)*. All three also display another Gothic hallmark, the pointed-arch window.

Another Gothic Revival example, this one more "irregular," is the *A. V. Peters House* in Eugene *(p. 11)*. It exhibits most of the distinguishing features of the Rural Gothic Cottage mode: steep-pitched roof, decorative eaves brackets, window hoods, and vertical, board-and-batten siding. As in the case of the houses at Forts Dalles and Simcoe, it was based on a design in an architectural pattern book. *Village and Farm Cottages* (1856 and 1869) was a collaboration between Henry Cleaveland, a well-known eastern architect, and the Backus Brothers, William and Samuel. The book followed the same general formula established by Downing and others, but its designs were specifically addressed to the working class. Moreover, it was an early exponent of the concept of mail-order architecture. A discreet notice at the back of the book advised readers that building plans and specifications for each featured design were available by mail for a mere four dollars, postpaid.

Similar asymmetric, "L"-shaped plans can be seen in the *Tom Crellin House* in Oysterville *(p 14)* and the *Episcopal Rectory* in the eastern Oregon town of Cove *(p. 15)*. The former has a number of stylistic touches that suggest it was not the work of an unaided vernacular builder. Its decorative features include flat-cut gingerbread trim on the gables, a hood mold over the second-story window, and a polygonal bay on the projecting wing. Similar conclusions can be made about the *Cove Rectory*, which was built under the direction of the Rev. R. D. Nevius. It features extremely steep gables, pointed windows, and vertical siding. According to research conducted by the late David Powers of the Oregon State Historic Preservation

Office, the plan was adapted from a design by a Portland architect, Albert H. Jordan.

As time passed, Gothic Revival houses began to adopt decorative features associated with other styles. The *Laughlin House* in the small town of Yamhill, southwest of Portland, illustrates some of these borrowings *(p. 17)*. The second story with its bargeboards, pointed windows, and steep gables is distinctly Gothic, while the first floor has a number of details—bays, decorative brackets, and horizontal shiplap siding—that are more commonly associated with the Italianate. Though distinct in theory, elements of these two styles were commonly mixed in both the literature and the building practice of the period.

A very different sort of Gothic can be found in downtown Portland. Perhaps because Downing and others had stressed the particular suitability of the Gothic Revival style for country living, it was never widely adopted in the city. The *Bishop's House (p. 2)* is a wonderful exception to the rule. Here the style has taken on urban trappings. Though it would seem to have little in common with the picturesque cottages Downing advocated, it is Gothic nonetheless in its allusions to the church architecture of its own century and, beyond that, to the medieval cathedrals of Europe. The overhanging roofs and asymmetrical configurations of its country cousins have necessarily been abandoned, but Gothic styling is apparent in the pointed arches and tracery of the third-floor windows and the steep-pitched false gable that rises above the roof line. In addition, the design—attributed to a French-trained San Francisco architect, Prosper Heurn—exploits its narrow city lot to achieve the upward-soaring spirit that virtually defines Gothic architecture.

Before leaving the Gothic Revival behind, we should mention the many wooden churches to be found in the Northwest. The *Old Church* in Portland, *Ascension Episcopal* in Cove, the two *St. Pauls* in Port Townsend and Port Gamble, and *First Presbyterian* in Jacksonville are particularly fine representatives of the style.

The Italianate

To judge by what has survived in the Pacific Northwest, the Italianate style was even more popular than the Gothic Revival. In part this may have been because Italianate houses were easier to build. Popularized on this side of the Atlantic by A. J. Downing and others, their prototypes were of Italian origin. Broadly they were of two types: rambling, "picturesque" villas, and more formal, symmetrical dwellings, which are sometimes designated as "Tuscan."

An example of the latter subtype is the *B. F. Dowell House* in Jacksonville *(p. 20)*. It illustrates how a few details can give a simple, rectangular house a stylistic identity. This house is "Tuscan" by virtue of its round-headed windows, classical portico, and frontal symmetry. The low-pitched, hipped roof was also typical of the style. The flat roofs prescribed for sunnier climates were often eschewed in the Northwest.

The basic rectangle could also be elaborated with bay windows set on both sides of a central portico. The *Baer House* in Baker City *(p. 21)*, the *Bergman House* in Portland *(p. 29)*, and the *McCall House* in Ashland *(p. 32)* illustrate the symmetrical, double-bay front. Larger, more elaborate versions of the same general idea can be found in the *Kirkman House* in Walla Walla and the *Bruce House* in nearby Waitsburg.

Dwellings of this type usually display several other defining characteristics of the Italianate: ornamental brackets beneath the eaves, segmental-arch windows, and elaborately carved window surrounds. Most of these decorative elements can also be found in asymmetrically configured structures. The *Isaac Woolen House* in Ashland *(p. 32)* for instance, combines these Italianate hallmarks with the "L"-shaped plan seen in the *Peters* and *Crellin* houses.

Even more asymmetrical and "irregular" (Downing's term) was the Italian Villa style. As exemplified by the Willamette Valley home of carpitect John Moyer *(p. 25)*, it typically had rambling bays and wings built around a central block that often extended into a tower. The resulting configuration was far more unpredictable and picturesque than symmetrically arranged Italianate houses. Even when the tower was left out, as in the *Jacob Jenne* and *John Kineth* houses in Coupeville *(p. 25)*, the asymmetrical plan helped free the Victorian house from its boxy past and paved the way for future developments.

Most of the Italianate houses that have survived in the Northwest are country or suburban dwellings: urban examples are fewer and farther between. One Seattle survivor is the *Ward House (p. 28)*, which demonstrates that even urban houses could have towers and picturesque mass. As for the classic bay-front Italianate townhouse that was so popular in San Francisco, they were relatively rare in the Northwest, though a few examples can still be seen in Portland and Astoria *(pp. 28, 29)*. More common than the urban townhouse was a larger, suburban variant—the gabled-ell cottage. This took the form of a tall, narrow, "L"-shaped house with a porch in the nook and a bay window on the projecting wing. Two examples, both of them pattern-book designs, are the *Ferguson* and *Keyes Houses (p. 34)* in Astoria and Bellingham. Another, the *Gerson House (p. 52)*, can be found in Port Townsend.

The Mansardic Styles

Of the various architectural styles popular in America in the Victorian period, the French Second Empire was a particular favorite of the upper middle class. Unlike the others it was not a revival style but a contemporary architectural movement. Born in France during the era of Louis Napoleon, it radiated an aura of modernity and continental elegance that appealed to those whose tastes – or pretensions – required more sophistication than houses in the Gothic or Italian manner. Its less elegant sobriquet, "The General Grant Style" derived from its frequent use in government buildings during and after the administration of the eighteenth president. *Villard Hall* on the University of Oregon Campus, and the *New Whatcom City Hall* in Bellingham are two such structures.

The best remaining example of a formal French Second Empire style residence in the region is Portland's *Jacob Kamm House (p. 38)*. Besides the mansard roof, it has several other features characteristic of the Second Empire: hooded, segmental-arch windows, round-topped dormers, paired entry doors, and a belt course that indicates on the outside the division of stories within the house. Though it doesn't look like it, the siding is wood, smoothly fitted, painted, and coigned to simulate masonry construction.

Another mansardic example, the *Frank Bartlett House (p. 42)* in Port Townsend, demonstrates that a sense of formal Second Empire styling can be achieved even on a small scale. But most other mansardic houses in Washington and Oregon belong to a more homey and casual subtype, the French Cottage. Examples include the *Captain Sawyer House (p. 42)*, a neighbor of the *Bartlett House*, and the *Zylstra House* in Coupeville *(p. 42)*, a one-story cottage with a jauntily curved mansard.

Tom Crellin House, Oysterville, 1869

Cottage, Port Gamble, c.1870

Libbey House, Coupeville, 1870

Hovander House, Ferndale, 1903

Ascension Episcopal Church and Rectory, Cove, 1875

This distinctive roof form was not merely a stylish device. It was also a practical way to add usable attic space to a structure. It thus offered itself as a way to enlarge as well as remodel existing houses. The *John Bunn House* in Yamhill *(p. 39)* is a good example of such an addition. The mansard added space as well as style to what probably started out as a vernacular farmhouse.

Other Second Empire survivors can be found scattered around Oregon and Washington, as witness the *Abel Eaton House* in Union *(p. 43)* and the *Hand House* in Albany. Even the army built at least one modest example—a small French cottage standing among the other buildings on Fort Vancouver's *Officers Row (p. 42)*. Nonetheless, the species is relatively rare today. Part of the reason was that later generations saw representatives of the General Grant Style as egregious white elephants and razed them with little hesitation whenever they seemed to stand in the way of progress.

The Stick Style

The Stick style, which gained popularity in the late 1870s, represented a turn back to the Gothic Revival. Indeed, Victorian architects sometimes referred to it as "Modern Gothic." Stick style houses generally had angular profiles with steep-pitched roofs and sharply pointed gables. Elaborate trusses and square towers were also common. But the defining characteristic of the style was a distinctive type of ornament that included thin vertical battens and stylized cross braces. According to Vincent Scully Jr., who coined the term, this patterning was an extension of the board-and-batten tradition of the Gothic Revival. The decorative posts, beams, and braces that adorned the outer skin of the structure pointed to and reflected the underlying frame that supported it.

The *Skipton House* in Albany *(p. 46)* illustrates some of these ideas. Designed by George Franklin Barber, a mail-order architect based in Knoxville, Tennessee, it shows both the stick patterning and angularity characteristic of the style. To these it adds some additional touches: lathe-turned spindlework on the porch and a sunburst panel above the second-story window. These were part of the so-called Eastlake style, a decorative mode often associated with the Stick style.

The term originally referred to the interior decorative motifs of the English designer, Charles Eastlake. Today, however, any incised or turned ornament produced with chisel and gouge is apt to be labeled "Eastlake." From the 1880s on, such decoration tended to replace the flat-cut gingerbread of earlier decades.

Another dwelling in Albany, the *Ralston House (p. 47)*, also exhibits Stick and Eastlake features. The bargeboards are finely detailed, and the facade has at least three variations of the sunburst. In addition, the thin battens atop the window hoods suggest, once again, the relationship between Stick style patterning and the Gothic Revival: they are strikingly similar to the ones that adorn the *Fort Dalles Surgeon's Quarters (p. 6)*.

Although pure examples of the Stick style are rare in the Pacific Northwest, the characteristic patterning was liberally applied to many late-nineteenth century dwellings, particularly those in the Queen Anne mode. A case in point is *Gaches Mansion* in La Connor *(p. 58)*, with its suggestions of Elizabethan half timbering.

The Queen Anne

If the Stick style was Gothic at root, it was also part of a stylistic continuum that led to a new revival style that took the country by storm in the mid 1880s—the Queen Anne. Its nominal prototypes were some boxy, eighteenth-century dwellings that first appeared during the reign of Queen Anne of England. Credit goes to the English designer William Norman Shaw for creating the Revival style; to Henry Hobson Richardson for bringing it across the Atlantic; and to a host of mostly unsung architects and builders for popularizing it across the length and breadth of the United States.

The Americanized version was an expansive, hipped-roof house with irregular massing and rambling, free-flowing floor plans. It often featured towers or turrets, fluted chimney stacks, leaded glass windows and an abundance of surface detail—stick patterning, turned spindlework, and shingles, to name three of the most common.

In the Pacific Northwest, no less than in the rest of the country, the corner-towered Queen Anne Villa became a staple of late nineteenth-century Victorian architecture. A textbook example is the *C.D. Drain House (p. 53)*, another design by the prolific G. F. Barber. But others abound throughout Oregon and Washington. Examples include the *Poulson House* in Portland, the *Hastings House* in Port Townsend *(back cover)*, and the *Fotheringham House*

Lee Laughlin House, Yamhill, 1879

in Spokane *(p. 56)*. Finally, Vancouver's nicely wrought and well proportioned *Marshall House (front cover)* shows that by century's end even the army had belatedly acquired a taste for the picturesque.

Meanwhile, the "classic" Queen Anne had begun flirtations with several other architectural modes. One of these was the Shingle style. Closely associated with exclusive seaside resorts in the Northeast, it never achieved wide acceptance in the rest of the country. But elements derived from it soon showed up in the work of good regional architects. An example in Port Townsend is the *J. C. Saunders House (p. 68)* by Edward A. Batwell. Although essentially Queen Anne, it has appropriated several Shingle style elements: shingle cladding, curved wall surfaces, and an oversized front gable. The "candle-snuffer" tower roof is from the Colonial Revival.

Another Washington house, *Wardner's Castle* in Bellingham *(p. 69)*, evokes the Shingle style even more forcefully. Long (and erroneously) attributed to the architects who designed the neighboring *Gamwell House*, the design is actually the work of the seminal Kirtland Cutter, whose career first blossomed in Spokane. As Henry Matthews, Cutter's biographer, notes, the *Wardner House* seems to have been inspired by *Kragsyde*, a Shingle style landmark in Massachusetts. Besides the same basic configuration, it borrows a number of specific details including the large, arched entry and generous second-story veranda.

Another branch of the Queen Anne led to the Classical Revival. When they had exhausted the stylistic repertoire of the Romantic Revival styles, architects and builders turned once again to the classical motifs they had mostly avoided for the past fifty years. Toward the end of the century, Queen Anne houses began to acquire stout turrets, Greco-Roman columns, Palladian windows and classical decorative motifs. These changes reflected the swing toward neoclassicism that occurred around the turn of the century. Hence the term "Free Classic" that is sometimes applied to late Queen Anne houses. Northwest examples include a number of dwellings in Washington: the *Schram House*, 1895 in Bellingham, the *Olsen House* in Vader *(p. 65)*, and the *Presby House* in Goldendale. To these add one in Clatskanie, Oregon, the *Flippin House (p. 72)*, whose twin Queen Anne towers flank a facade composed in classical symmetry.

A final Queen Anne example, the *Gamwell House* in Bellingham

(p. 64), also deserves mention. Designed by Longstaff and Black, a pair of Boston architects, it was built for a real estate speculator during Fairhaven's heady boom period in the late 1880s. With its restless curves, numerous verandas, art glass windows, and exotic tower, it points to an order of opulence and eccentricity that has almost completely disappeared from the American scene. Vintage photographs show that similarly appointed houses on an even larger scale dominated the larger cities of the Pacific Northwest in the 1890s. Since then, however, almost all have succumbed to the demands of progress.

The Eclectic Age

As we have seen, the romantic revival styles of the early Victorian era provided models for later architectural developments. Once the precedent of borrowing from the past had been firmly established, architects rummaged freely through the attic of history in search of new prototypes. Evidently many of them felt free to mix, match and incorporate details from the preceding romantic styles to create entirely new stylistic syntheses.

One of these was the new Romanesque style pioneered by the great American architect, Henry Hobson Richardson. An example in this mode is Portland's *MacKenzie House (p. 73)*. Designed by Whidden and Lewis, it exhibits several hallmarks of the style: massive construction in stone, a stout tower with a conical cap, and rounded Roman arches in the arcade that encloses the front porch. Another house that shares some of these elements is *Hoquiam's Castle. (p. 77)*. Though of frame construction, it has a raised foundation of massive stones, a round tower, and a porch enclosed by an arcade. With an eclecticism typical of the turn of the century, this house also exhibits various Queen Anne and Shingle elements.

The "Richardsonian Romanesque," which in its purest form required expensive masonry construction, was never widely popular, but it did gain some currency as a high style for the well-to-do. Another elite style, the Chateauesque, which found its greatest American exponent in Richard Morris Hunt, derived from the great fifteenth and sixteenth-century chateaux of France's Loire Valley. An unlikely specimen in the Pacific Northwest is Port Townsend's *Eisenbeis House (p. 76)*. Built by a former German baker, it has the overall configuration and many of the features associated with the style: masonry construction, semi-circular towers and turrets, a steep roof, and a roof line complicated with shaped dormers, high-flying chimney stacks, and pinnacles. Needless to say, such expensive trappings did not often invite vernacular imitations.

Another late nineteenth-century dwelling with exotic overtones can be found in Spokane. Charged with the task of creating the most impressive residence west of the Mississippi, Kirtland Cutter designed a remarkable mansion for mining speculator Patrick "Patsy" Clark *(p. 80)*. Although quite original in conception, the house employs a range of "Moorish" decorative motifs and structural elements inside and out. But even without these, the effect of the free-flowing plan and the striking color scheme—warm-yellow brick, brown sandstone trim, and red metal roof tiles—are quite extraordinary. If not the most impressive house west of the Mississippi, Clark's residence must rank as a clear contender.

Cutter's foray into Islamic exotica may have been uncharacteristic of his other work, but it was entirely consonant with the tenor of the times. As late as the 1890s owners and architects were still indulging a taste for architectural fantasy. A case in point is *Piggot's Castle* in Portland *(p.77)*. Perched on a hill on the southwest side of town, it is an unlikely and ultimately unclassifiable blend of elements that some identify as Moorish, Norman, and Romanesque.

Just a few years later, however, such experiments had become rare and unfashionable. In the waning years of the nineteenth century a less effusive, more sober spirit had begun to assert itself, and by the first years of the twentieth it had become the dominant note. Houses based on the old models continued to be built for several years after the turn of the century, but they seldom ventured again into the pure fancy that characterized Victorian design at its height. The death of Queen Victoria in 1901 was merely the symbolic end of an architectural era that had in fact ended several years earlier.

B.F. Dowell House, Jacksonville, 1861

Baer House, Baker City, 1882

Victorian Guide

Oregon and Washington

This section contains a brief guide to Pacific Northwest communities where Victorian architecture flourished and has survived. It is certainly not exhaustive, but it should serve to point interested parties in the right direction.

In some areas, researchers may wish to consult books and local guides that offer more detailed information than can be included here. These days even small towns commonly issue maps, brochures, and walking tours that highlight their architecture. The bibliography on page 78 may be of help in this regard.

A few notes on what follows:
• Houses and other buildings illustrated in this book are marked with bullets and page references.
• When possible we have included phone numbers for those structures that are open to the public. In making plans to visit it would be wise to call ahead.
• Except as noted, the listed houses should be assumed to be private residences. It should go without saying that visitors should respect the privacy of the occupants.

Oregon

Although assorted explorers, fur traders, and missionaries established outposts early in the nineteenth century, real settlement of the Oregon Territory did not begin until the 1840s when the first pioneer wagon trains began to arrive. In those early years most settlement occurred along the banks of the Columbia and Willamette, and it is there that much of the state's oldest architecture is to be found today. Development along the coast, in the mountains, and in the great eastern plateau that makes up two thirds of the state came later in the century.

Albany

Located at the confluence of the Willamette and Calapooia Rivers, Albany was founded in 1848 when the Monteith brothers, Walter and Thomas, arrived from upstate New York and purchased the site from the Hacklemans who had arrived a few years earlier. For the next several decades, the settlement grew steadily as it became by turns a riverboat landing, stage stop, and railroad center. By the late 1880s, it was an important agricultural, manufacturing, and shipping hub. In the twentieth century, however, it lost much of its economic basis when highways supplanted rail and river transportation. As a result, Albany has been able to preserve more than three-hundred Victorian houses, churches, and commercial buildings in its three historic districts.

Downtown Historic District:
Comprising mostly commercial buildings, the district is bounded by the Willamette River, Montgomery, Washington and 5th Streets.

Flinn Block, 1889. 222 1st SW. The mansard roof that originally capped this Second Empire commercial building was damaged by fire and removed in 1911, but some interesting details, incuding fine cast iron work, remain.

Albany Farm Supply, 1887. 136 Lyon. Architect: Warren H. Williams. Originally the S.E. Young store, this Italianate commercial building was the work of the same architect who designed the *Morris Marks House* in Portland and *Craigdarrock Castle* in Victoria, B.C.

Conn & Huston Grocery, 1893. 208-210 1st SW. A brick commercial building with cast iron pilaster, sloped parapet and a variety of window shapes.

Hackleman District

Located on the east side of town, the district is roughly bounded by Pacific Blvd., Lyons, 2nd, and Madison Streets.

• **Ralston House,** 1889. 632 Baker SE. Insurance man John Ralston had come to Oregon by covered wagon when he was a boy. As an adult, he built one of the best examples of Eastlake styling remaining in the Pacific Northwest. *p. 47.*

Chamberlain House, 1884. 208 7th SE. This Stick style residence, the tallest house in Albany, was built for George E. Chamberlain, an attorney who served Oregon both as governor and U. S. Senator.

William Hand House, c.1886. 319 7th SE. A vernacular house with a mansard roof.

• **George Hochstedler House,** c.1889. 237 6th SE. Architect: G. F. Barber. Based on design No. 41 in Barber's *Cottage Souvenir No. 2,* (1891) this Stick style house was originally the home of George Hochstedler, an Albany building contractor and planing-mill operator. It reportedly cost $6000 to build. *p. 46.*

• **Goltra House,** 1893. 331 Montgomery SE. The Italianate home of William H. Goltra, a New Jerseyite who walked all the way from Missouri to Oregon in 1852. *p. 25.*

• **Frank Skipton House,** c.1895. 416 4th Ave SE. Architect: G. F. Barber. A Stick style house based on Design No. 11 in G. F. Barber's *Cottage Souvenir No. 2.* According to the latter: "Cost to build, as per description, $1,400." *p. 46.*

Wolverton House, c.1889. 810 Lyon SE. The Italianate residence of Charles E. Wolverton who served as an Oregon Supreme Court Justice.

Beam House, 1878. 508 5th. A good example of the Stick style.

Monteith District

The boundaries of this district west of downtown are 2nd, Lyon, 12th, and Elm Streets.

Baltimore House, c.1891. 632 Washington. A restrained residence adorned minimally with Stick-style cross bracing.

• **L. C. Marshall House,** c.1895. 540 6th SW. An ample Queen Anne residence that was originally the home of the president of the Albany Butter and Produce Company. *p. 57.*

Train House, 206 7th SW. Queen Anne. Now the *Brier Rose Inn.*

541 926-0345.

Whitespires Church, 1891. 510 5th SW. Architect: Walter Pugh. A large Gothic Revival church with a square, castellated spire and Povey stained glass from Portland.

St. Mary's Catholic Church, 1899. 820 S. Ellsworth. The design is attributed to Father Louis Matayer, a French priest who evidently modeled it on Gothic and Romanesque originals in Europe.

Mason House, 1883. 538 SW 6th. A French Second Empire house that originally belonged to Albany druggist David Mason.

Armstrong-Jones House, c.1869. 516 Elm. Once a stage coach stop, this Gothic Revival house received some Eastlake refurbishing in the 1890s.

Ashland

Long before it became famous for its Shakespeare Festival, Ashland prospered as an agricultural center. Located at the foot of the Klamath Range, near the California border, it was (and still is) a convenient stop on the long road between Sacramento and Portland. Many of its surviving Victorian homes have become bed and breakfasts.

Chappell-Swedenburg House Museum, c.1900. 990 Siskiyou at Mountain. A large, early twentieth-century house with some Victorian features. It is now an Oregon Historical Society museum.

• **Woolen House,** 1876. 131 North Main. An "L"-shaped Italianate house with elaborate eaves brackets and an uncharacteristically steep roof. It was the retirement home of Isaac Woolen, a prosperous Bear Creek Valley farmer. *p. 32.*

• **W. H. Atkinson House,** 1880. 125 North Main. This house was built for W. F. Atkinson, an English émigré. The brackets and pendants on the porch and below the cornices are similar to those on the Woolen House next door. It is now a bed and breakfast. **541 482-0220.** *p. 32.*

Pedigrift House, 1888. 407 Scenic Drive. A symmetrical, double-bay, raised-basement structure with Queen Anne elements. This house type is more commonly found in Northern California. It is now a bed and breakfast. **541 482-1888.**

• **McCall House,** 1883. 153 Oak. Builder: L. S. P. Marsh. A double-bay Italianate house, reminiscent of the Marks and Bergman Houses

Alonzo Brown House, Oakland, 1888

Moyer House, Brownsville, c.1881

Goltra House, Albany, 1893

Kineth House, Coupeville, 1887

Jacob Jenne House, Coupeville, c.1889

in Portland. It was originally the home of John McCall, whose varied career included mining, farming, store keeping, flour milling, horse soldiering, wool processing, and—as a member of the state legislature—law making. The house is now a bed and breakfast. **541 482-9296**. *p. 32*.

Queen Anne House, c.1895. Granite near High. An interesting mixture of elements including Stick-Eastlake braces and cutouts, Italianate cornice brackets, and a semi-octagonal Queen Anne Bay.

Henry B. Carter House, 1888. 91 Gresham. A large Queen Anne house with Stick style elements. It was built by banker and businessman H. B. Carter. Beautifully restored it is now the *Antique Rose Inn*. **541 482-6285**.

Queen Anne House, c.1895. 364 Vista. Queen Anne tending toward the Shingle style.

Astoria

Founded as a fur trading outpost in 1811, Astoria did not begin to develop as a permanent settlement until the 1840s when the first American wagon trains began arriving in Oregon. The town's location at the mouth of the Columbia, between Puget Sound and San Francisco, endowed it admirably for its principal nineteenth-century activities—shipping, logging, and salmon canning. The town has managed to retain a good sampling of the Victorian homes constructed during that prosperous period in its history.

• **Flavel Mansion,** 1885. 441 8th at Duane. Architect: C. W. Leick. Built by a shipping magnate, Captain George Flavel, this High Victorian Queen Anne is now the home of the Clatsop County Historical Museum and is open for public tours. Leick was the architect of several West Coast lighthouses. **503 325-2203**. *p. 35*.

Hiram Brown House, 1852. 1337 Franklin. This house, one of the oldest residences in Oregon, displays traces of the Gothic Revival. The original owner was Hiram Brown, a river pilot.

John Hobson House, 1863. 469 Bond. A Vernacular Victorian with strong Gothic Revival roots. Hobson, an Englishman by birth, came west with the Whitman-Applegate party in the early 1840s.

• **Page House,** 1879. 1393 Franklin Ave. A long, narrow Italianate townhouse that would have been at home in San Francisco. It was a gift from Hiram Brown to his daughter on the occasion of her wedding to Judge Charles Page. *p. 28*.

• **Benjamin Young House,** 1888. 3652 Duane. The Queen Anne home of a Swedish immigrant who made his fortune in the salmon-packing industry. It is now the *Benjamin Young Inn*. **503 325-6172**. *p. 46*.

• **Holmes House,** 1890. 682 34th. Gust Holmes, a Swedish fisherman whose hard work eventually made him a salmon cannery owner, built this eclectic Queen Anne house on what was then called Holmes Hill. *p. 49*.

Nellie Wilson House, 1895. 1243 Franklin. A vernacular Queen Anne abundantly endowed with Eastlake porch spindlework.

Peter L. Cherry House, 1883. 836 15th. An Italianate dwelling that served the British Consul during the period when Astoria was a major port of entry.

• **Albert W. Ferguson House,** 1886. 1661 Grand. Albert W. Ferguson, a local carpitect, evidently adapted a plan from *Bicknell's Detail, Cottage, and Constructive Architecture* in designing his own home. The same plan was used for the *Keyes House* in Bellingham, Washington. *p. 34*.

Sanborn House, 1890. 1711 Grand. Queen Anne with a nod or two to the Shingle style. George C. Sanborn, its first owner, also owned a canning-plant.

• **Martin Foard House,** 1892. 690 17th. The original owner was one of the proprietors of the Foard and Stokes Mercantile and Furniture store. *p. 65*.

Baker City

Remnants of the Oregon trail can be found just a few miles east of town, but Baker City owes its existence to an 1861 gold strike that drew a flood of prospectors and camp followers to northeastern Oregon. It is said that it once rivaled Spokane and Boise in population, a claim that is bolstered by the nice collection of Victorian homes that remain from its heyday. The Baker Historic District runs along Main Street from Madison to Estes.

• **Baer House,** 1882. 2333 Main. A double-bay Italianate house that was originally the residence of a local merchant. Its neighbor, the *Adler House*, a few doors south, is nearly identical in configuration. *The Baer House* is now a bed and breakfast. **541 524-1912**. *p. 21*.

Adler House, c.1882. 2305 Main. The other half of the pair of Italianate houses that bracket this block. It was once the home of Leo Adler, who reportedly left $20,000,000 to Baker County when he died. His former home has been restored and refurbished with its original Victorian furniture. **800 523-1235.**

• **Ison House,** 1887. 1790 Washington. A towered Queen Anne in brick that has been recycled for use as a bank building. *p. 60.*

Queen Anne House, 1701 Washington. Queen Anne with Stick and Eastlake details.

Clark House, 1522 Washington Ave. A restrained Italianate house with an asymmetrically placed entry and a two-story bay window.

Queen Anne House, 2336 2nd. Restrained Queen Anne.

St. Francis deSales Cathedral, 2235 1st at Church. A large Gothic-Romanesque church in rough-cut stone, with twin steeple towers and pointed-arch windows.

Brownsville

• **Moyer House,** c.1881. 204 Main. The home and creation of carpenter and mill owner John M. Moyer, this Italianate villa was restored by the Linn County Historical Society. It is now a part of the county museum system. Brownsville is located east of I-5, between Albany and Eugene. *p. 25.*

Canby

In addition to a vintage depot that has survived from the days of the Oregon & California Railroad, several late nineteenth-century houses can be found in or near this small community on the Willamette.

Barlow House, 1885. 24670 S. Hwy 99E. A symmetrical, double-bay Italianate house that has been recently restored.

Herman Anthony Farm, 1891. 10205 S. New Era Rd. A Queen Anne farmhouse.

William Knight House, 1875. 525 SW 4th. A two-story, rectangular residence in the Federal style.

Canyon City

St. Thomas Episcopal Church, 1876. 135 Washington. Another Gothic Revival church thought to have been built by the Rev. R. D. Nevius who also built *Episcopal Church and Rectory* in Cove. Canyon City, which is located just south of John Day on U. S. 395, also has the *Herman and Eliza Oliver Historical Museum* and the cabin of Oregon poet Joaquin Miller.

Clatskanie

• **Flippin House,** 1899. 620 Tichenor. Builders: Markwell and Sons. The home of Thomas J. Flippin, a logger and sawmill operator, this late Victorian, Classical Revival house was restored eighty years later by *Clatskanie Senior Citizens* and is open for tours by the public. Clatskanie is located near the Columbia River, about thirty-five miles east of Astoria on U. S. Hwy. 30. *p. 72.*

Coos Bay

Tower-Flanagan House, 1872. 476 Newmark. Victorian Gothic Revival. Founded as Marshfield in 1854, Coos Bay is located about twenty miles north of Coquille. A few miles up the coast highway is the *Umpqua River Lighthouse* built in 1894.

Coquille

Incorporated in the mid 1880s, Coquille is a timber and retirement town located on State Route 42, a few miles inland and south of Coos Bay. Also of note is the *Coquille River Lighthouse (1895)* in nearby Bandon.

• **Sherwood House,** 1901. 257 E. Main. Architect: G. F. Barber. Andrew J. Sherwood, an attorney and businessman, built his expansive Queen Anne villa using plans supplied by the Knoxville, Tennessee mail-order architect. *p. 55.*

Harlocker House, 1891. 18 S. Collier St. Architect: Attributed to G. F. Barber. Queen Anne.

Paulson House, 1906. 86 N. Dean. A large Queen Anne residence in the Free-Classic manner. Note the broad gables, classical porch posts, and stout corner tower.

Corvallis

The town got its start in 1846-48 when pioneer Joseph C. Avery cleared twelve acres of land near the confluence of the Willamette and Mary's Rivers. In time it became the Benton County seat and

Page House, Astoria, 1879

Ward House, Seattle, 1882

Bergman House, Portland, 1885

Italianate Townhouse, Portland, 1880

29

home to Oregon State University. Some interesting Victoriana remains from its early years.

Benton County Courthouse, 1888. 120 NW 4th St. Architect: Delos D. Neer. High Victorian Italianate.

• **James Wilson House,** 1891. 340 SW 5th. Architect: Bushrod Washington Wilson. Queen Anne with unusual gable ends. *p. 51.*

Kline House, 1885. 308 NW 8th. The Italianate home of Lewis Kline, a tailor who arrived in Corvallis in 1864 and later founded a dry goods store.

J.R. Bryson House, 1882. 242 NW 7th. A cross-gabled Italianate villa that seems to have undergone some modification.

Hadley-Locke House, 1893. 704 NW 9th. Queen Anne.

Helm-Hout House, c.1895. 844 SW 5th. Queen Anne.

Pernot House, 1896. 242 SW 5th. Queen Anne.

Cove

• **Ascension Episcopal Church and Rectory,** 1875. Church St. Architect: attributed to Albert H. Jordan. A pair of matching Gothic Revival structures with steep gables and vertical board-and-batten siding. The church even has stylized wooden buttresses. The Rev. R. D. Nevius who directed the construction, is believed to have adapted this church plan from a design intended for one in Walla Walla. Cove is located not far from Union, at the foot of eastern Oregon's Wallowa Mountains. *p. 15.*

Drain

The town was founded in 1872 when C. D. Drain, a former homesteader and soon-to-be state senator, donated sixty acres of Douglas County land to the Oregon & California Railroad "in consideration of establishing a station...and laying out a town to be called 'Drain.'" In the years that followed, it flourished as a timber center and railroad shipping point. It is nestled on the eastern edge of the Coast Range, west of I-5, between Roseburg and Eugene.

• **C.D. Drain House,** c.1891. 100 E. Main. Architect: G. F. Barber. The plan for this house appears as Design No. 37 in Barber's *Cottage Souvenir No. 2.* Nearly identical houses can be found in Eureka Springs, Arkansas and Annapolis, Maryland. This one now

serves as an office building of the local school district. *p. 53.*

• **Hassard House,** c.1900. 105 A. Charles E. Hassard, the original owner, was a railroad carpenter and farmer who also served as the U. S. land commissioner in the area. The plan and many of the details seem to have been based on Design No. 33 in G. F. Barber's *Cottage Souvenir No. 2. p. 55.*

Eugene

The town was platted in 1852 and named after Eugene Skinner, the first settler in the area. Located at the nether end of the Willamette Valley, it became a lumber and agricultural center as well as the home of the University of Oregon. Today much of the town's surviving nineteenth-century architecture can be found in the Skinner's Butte Historical District and adjacent neighborhoods.

• **Shelton-McMurphey-Johnson House,** 1888. 303 Willamette. Architect: Walter D. Pugh; Builder: Nels Roney. Baronially situated on Skinner's Butte, overlooking the railroad depot and the rest of town, this High-Victorian Queen Anne castle was built for Dr. T. W. Shelton at a cost of $7,000. It has been saved, thanks in large part to benefactor Dr. Eva Johnson. It is now owned by the City of Eugene and is available for tours. **541 484-0808.** *p.63*

Watts House, 1893. 335 Pearl. Although built by lumberman J. N. B. Fuller, this house bears the name of Eugene's first optometrist. In recent years it has been recycled for commercial use.

Deady Hall, 1876. U of O Campus. Architect: William W. Piper. This French Second Empire style structure once constituted the entire university.

Villard Hall, 1885. U of O Campus. Architect: Warren H. Williams. This mansard-roofed academic building, with hints of the Chateauesque style, was financed by the railroad and financial magnate, Henry Villard.

Collier House, 1885. 14th and University. Once the home of a science professor, this Italianate residence now serves as the *University of Oregon Faculty Club.*

• **A. V. Peters House,** c.1870. 1611 Lincoln. Architects: Henry Cleaveland and William and Samuel Backus. Based on design No. 12 in *Village and Farm Cottages* (1856 and 1869), this board-and-batten house is one of the best surviving examples of the picturesque rural Gothic style in the Northwest. *p. 11.*

• **Chambers House,** c.1895. Taylor at 10th. The Queen Anne home of Frank Chambers, a businessman and Eugene booster who helped found local opera and theater companies. *p. 50.*

Smith House, c.1898. 2065 Lincoln. Queen Anne.

Heceta Head

Named for Bruno Heceta, a Portuguese explorer who charted the area for Spain in 1775, Heceta Head juts into the ocean about midway down the Oregon coast, a location that makes one of the most picturesque settings for a lighthouse in the United States. Twelve miles south on Hwy. 101, the town of Florence has several turn-of-the-century commercial buildings in its Old Town District.

• **Heceta House,** 1894. 92072 Hwy. 101. A double house in a restrained Queen Anne mode. Originally built for the light keepers and their families, the house was restored in the 1980s and is now maintained by the National Forest Service. Today it serves both as a bed and breakfast and an interpretive center. The light tower itself, with its small duty station, stands at the edge of the headland. **541-547-3696.** *p. 59.*

Jacksonville

In 1851 a gold strike on southern Oregon's Jackson Creek created a town almost overnight. Although the gold played out within a decade or two, Jacksonville continued in relative prosperity until the end of the nineteenth century when it was eclipsed in population and political importance by neighboring Medford. As a result, the town has remained largely unspoiled and today contains a fine legacy of historical architecture. Besides two interesting churches and dozens of well-preserved houses, it boasts an authentic main street lined with brick commercial buildings. More evidence of early gold mining activity can be seen in nearby Gold Hill.

McCully House, 1861. 240 E. California. The Gothic Revival home of John W. McCully, one of Jacksonville's earliest physicians. Now a restaurant and inn. **541 899-1942.**

• **Nunan House,** c.1892. 635 N. Oregon. Architect: G. F. Barber. Dry goods merchant Jeremiah Nunan used one of Barber's fanciest plans to build this large house. Beautifully restored, it is a private dwelling but open for public tours. *p. 54.*

Beekman House, 1875. 325 E. California at 7th. Once the home of Cornelius C. Beekman, a Wells Fargo agent and banker, the house is now a museum. **541 773-6536.**

• **B. F. Dowell House,** 1861. 5th and F. A remarkable brick Italianate house in the formal Tuscan mode. Probably inspired by a pattern-book design, it was built by Benjamin Franklin Dowell, a lawyer who became a merchant during Jacksonville's gold rush. It remains a private residence. *p. 20.*

First Presbyterian Church, 1881. California at 6th. Essentially Gothic with some Eastlake touches. The stained glass windows are said to be from Italy.

Herman Helms House, 1878. 320 Oregon at Pine. The Italianate home of Herman Helms, a baker and the original owner of the Table Rock Saloon.

John Day

Adventist Church, 1878. 261 W. Main. A fine Victorian Gothic Revival church with serpentine bargeboards inspired, some say, by desert rattlers. The design and the carving have been attributed to Samuel Hope. John Day is located at the junction of U. S. 395 and Route 7 near Canyon City. It was named for a scout who served with the Astor exploration of 1811. History buffs might also be interested in the Kam Wah Chung Museum, which features exhibits on Chinese and western herbal medicine.

Klamath Falls

• **Goeller House,** c.1905. 234 Riverside Dr. Architect: G. F. Barber. Carpenter and mill operator Fred Goeller based his Queen Anne style house on plan No. 56 in Barber's *Cottage Souvenir No. 2.* Klamath Falls is located 76 miles east of Medford. *p. 55.*

Lakeview

Lakeview was established in 1876, ninety-six miles east of Klamath Falls.

Queen Anne House, c.1895. 170 G. A corner-towered Queen Anne that has been restored and painted in recent years.

Isaac Woolen House, Ashland, 1876

Asahel Bush House, Salem, 1878

John McCall House, Ashland, 1883

W.H. Atkinson House, Ashland, 1880

Chandler House, 1905. Center and H. Queen Anne.

Schminck Memorial Museum, 128 South E. A small museum featuring remnants of early pioneer life.

Milton-Freewater

Still-Perkins House, 1883. 112 SE 6th. A cottage with Stick and Eastlake details. The town is located south of Walla Walla on State Route 11.

Molalla

Horace Dibble House, 1859. 616 S. Molalla. A well-preserved Colonial saltbox. Molalla is east of Woodburn, between Oregon City and Silverton.

Newberg

Like other towns on the Willamette River, Newberg was founded when American settlers began to pour into the valley in the 1840s. Today it takes pride in a number of well-preserved Victorian houses that reflect its early history and Quaker heritage. Also of note is *Champoeg State Park* in nearby St. Paul, seven miles southeast of Newberg on the Willamette River. The park's attractions include replicas of a pioneer cabin and the Gothic-inspired home of mountain man Robert Newell.

Hoover-Minthorne House, 1881. 115 S. River St. This Italianate house, the boyhood home of President Herbert Hoover, is thought to be the oldest residence in town. It is now a house museum, offering group tours by appointment.

Baptist Parsonage, c.1890. 315 N. College. The church itself has long since departed.

Moore House, c.1890. 911 E. 3rd. One of the three surviving Italianate houses in Newberg.

C. L. Sloan House, 1896. 801 E. 3rd. Queen Anne.

Jesse Edwards House, 1892. 402 S. College. The Stick-Eastlake home of local builder and landowner Jesse Edwards.

Mills House, 1895. 201 S. College. Restrained Queen Anne.

• **Robert Newell House**, 1852. 8089 Champoeg Rd. NE. This house is a 1959 restoration of the original Gothic Revival home of Robert "Doc" Newell, a trapper and mountain man who brought the first covered wagon west to the Willamette Valley. **503 678-5537.** *p. 10.*

Oakland

The first permanent white settlement in the Umpqua Valley was founded in 1846 when winter stranded a group of Willamette-bound settlers. After the Oregon & California Railroad arrived in 1872, the town enjoyed a modest boom that lasted until the turn of the century and beyond. Today, as befits a National Historic District, it retains a distinct nineteenth-century flavor.

• **Alonzo Brown House**, 1888. 208 Chestnut. The stylish Italianate residence of one of the town's founders. *p. 24.*

Z. L. Dimmick House, 1893. 114 N.E. 7th. Restrained Queen Anne.

A. Geary Young House, 1895. 5th and Walnut. Queen Anne.

Oregon City

As one of the oldest American communities on the Pacific side of the mountains, Oregon City is heir to a rich legacy of nineteenth-century building. It was founded in the 1830s by representatives of the British Hudson's Bay Company and in the pioneer era became the focus of American settlement in the Oregon Territory. Although post-World War II suburbanization and commercial encroachment have exacted a considerable toll on its historic resources, the town has maintained a representative sampling of its early architecture—including some rare representatives of the Federal, Greek, and Gothic Revival styles, many of them located in the McLoughlin Neighborhood.

• **E. B. Fellows House**, 1867. 416 S. McLoughlin. A center-gabled Gothic Revival house built by Capt. Fellows, an engineer and riverboat builder. *p. 10.*

• **Gray-Hackett House**, 1894. 415 17th St. Queen Anne with a square side tower. Built for a school teacher, George Gray, this house later became the residence of Edward Hackett, once mayor of Oregon City. In recent years it has been used for commercial space. *p. 50.*

McLoughlin House, 1846. Center and 7th. The Georgian-style home of the chief factor of the Hudson's Bay Company.

F. A. Toepplemann House, c.1880. 306 McLoughlin Promenade. This diminutive vernacular Victorian was a rental property of local landowner F. A. Toepplemann.

Ferguson House, Astoria, 1886

Keyes House, Bellingham, 1892

Flavel Mansion, Astoria, 1885

Captain Ainsworth House, 1851. 19195 S. Leland Rd. The best example in the Northwest of a Greek Revival temple-form house. It was originally the home of John C. Ainsworth, a steamship pilot who became president of several transportation companies in the area. It is now a museum.

• **Edward Howell House,** c.1885. 712 12th. Howell started out as a railroad conductor but became a real estate developer. His residence contains many Eastlake touches. The design is said to have been based on a plan in a pattern book. *p. 51.*

• **Milne House,** c.1869. 224 Center. James Milne, a carpenter by trade, built this center-gabled Gothic Revival house for his own residence. *p. 10.*

• **Huntley House,** 1896. 916 Washington. Queen Anne with Eastlake spindlework decoration. Note how the front gable intersects the corner tower. *p. 49.*

Charles Babcock House, 1892. 1214 Washington. Queen Anne.

Harvey Cross House, c.1885. 809 Washington. Italianate.

Port Orford Vicinity

Hughes House, 1898. Cape Blanco State Park, 10 miles north of Port Orford. Builder: Per Johan Lindberg. This was the home of Patrick Hughes, an Irish immigrant who came to Oregon looking for gold but was more successful in acquiring land and raising dairy cattle. Maintained by the Oregon State Parks Division, it is open to the public from April through October.

Portland

Thanks to its strategic location near the confluence of the Columbia and Willamette Rivers, Portland, which was founded in the early 1840s, soon became the largest city in Oregon. Though it has prospered and grown since its earliest beginnings, it has also managed to retain an excellent, if widely scattered, collection of nineteenth-century architecture. Many of its early commercial buildings are conveniently clustered in the Yamhill Historic District downtown. But its surviving Victorian houses are spread out to the north and south and on both sides of the Willamette River.

Portland SW

Reed House, 1887. 2036 SW Main. Architect: Otto Kleeman. A duplex in the Queen Anne style.

Cardwell-Parrish House, 1888. 7543 SW Fulton Park Blvd. Architect: Robert W. Shoppell. A corner-towered Queen Anne, with stick work in the gables and Eastlake spindlework on the porches and balconies.

The Old Church, 1883. 1422 SW 11th at Clay. Architect: Warren Heywood Williams. A large and impressive Gothic Revival church by the architect who designed Portland's *Marks House*, Eugene's *Villard Hall*, and Victoria's *Craigdarrock Castle*. It is open to the public for self-guided tours. **503 222-2031.**

Catherine White House, 1893. 1924 SW 14th. A nicely maintained Queen Anne house perched on one of the hills in southwest Portland.

Morris Marks House, 1882. 1501 SW Harrison. Architect: Warren H. Williams. Located in a hilly neighborhood in southwest Portland, this double-bay Italianate house has been beautifully restored in recent years. It was designed and built for Portland shoe merchant Marks, an immigrant from Poland.

• **Italianate Townhouse,** 1880. 1134 SW 12th. A bay-front townhouse that also belonged to Morris Marks. *p. 29.*

• **Jacob Kamm House,** 1871. 1425 SW 20th. Architect: Attributed to Justen Krumbein; Builder: L. Therkelsen. The best surviving example of the formal French Second Empire style in the Northwest, the *Kamm House* first belonged to a Swiss immigrant who made his fortune in river transportation. Restored in the twentieth century, it is now in use as an office building. *p. 38.*

• **Piggot's Castle,** 1892. 2591 SW Buckingham Terrace. A three-story brick and frame "castle" with Norman, Romanesque and Moorish influences. Also known as *Gleaal Castle*, it was built by Charles Henry Piggot, a lumberman and brick yard owner. *p. 77.*

• **The Bishop's House,** 1879. 219 SW Stark. Architect: Prosper Huerne. A rare and remarkable example of High Victorian Gothic styling put to domestic use in an urban setting. Constructed of brick, stucco and cast iron, it was once a church chancellery but now serves as a commercial building. *p. 2.*

Portland SE

James Polhemus House, c.1900. 135 SE 16th. Queen Anne.

• **Poulson House,** 1895. 3040 SE McLoughlin Blvd. A large and impressive Queen Anne House. Built by lumber baron Johan Poulson at the foot of the Ross Island Bridge, it has since been recycled for commercial use. *p. 59.*

W. E. Brainard House, 1888. 5332 SE Morrison. A double-bay Italianate house.

R. Hawthorne House, 1892. 1007 SE 12th. Architect: David McKeen. Queen Anne.

Kendall House, 1889. 3908 SE Taggart at 39th. Architect: Joseph Kendall. Architect Kendall designed and built this ambitious Queen Anne-Romanesque house for himself. Romanesque features includes round-headed arches and a bay of rough-hewn ashlar that sets off the brick construction elsewhere in the house.

Portland NW

• **MacKenzie House,** 1894. 615 NW 20th Ave. Architects: William Whidden and Ion Lewis. A three-story mansion of stone built by Dr. K. A. J. MacKenzie who founded the University of Oregon Medical School. The design, by Boston architects Whidden and Lewis, is Richardsonian Romanesque with a few nods to the Shingle style. *p. 73.*

• **Goldsmith House,** 1896. 1116 NW 24th. A Stick style suburban house. Note the three different types of decorative trusses in the gables. *p. 52.*

• **Bergman House,** 1885. 2134 NW Hoyt. A symmetrical, double-bay Italianate house similar to the Morris Marks House. It was originally owned by Joseph Bergman, a Portland butcher. *p. 29.*

Nathan Loeb House, 1890. 726 NW 22nd. Queen Anne with a range of exterior Eastlake ornament.

Campbell Townhouses, 1893. NW 17th and Irving. Builder: Daniel F. Campbell. A row of attached, Queen Anne townhouses.

Tanner House, 1893. 2248 NW Johnson. Queen Anne.

Trenkman Houses, 1890. NW 17th, 18th and Hoyt. Architect: Herman Trenkman. A row of five gabled-ell cottages in the Queen Anne style.

Union Station, 1894. Foot of NW 6th. Architect: Van Brunt and Howe. Portland's classic, Richardsonian Romanesque train station.

Portland NE

• **John Palmer House,** 1890. 4314 N. Mississippi. Builder-contractor John Palmer built this Eastlake-detailed Queen Anne house on Portland's northeast side. Besides the elaborate gablework and horseshoe-arched porch braces, it features Povey stained glass and a fine collection of Victorian furniture. It is now a bed and breakfast. **503 284-5893.** *p. 61.*

Freiwald House, 1906. 1810 NE 15th. A corner-towered, "Edwardian" Queen Anne villa with classical-revival elements. It was built by Gustav E. Freiwald, a real estate speculator.

Groat-Gates House, 1892. 35 NE 22nd. A large Queen Anne house.

Queen Anne House, 3257 SE Hawthorne.

Roseburg

The largest city in Douglas County first assumed importance as an agricultural and timber center in the 1890s. Besides the usual assortment of restored villas and manses that once housed former mayors and other prominent citizens, the town has managed to preserve some of its early vernacular housing as well. This is unusual, for such houses are frequently among the first to be razed or remodeled in the interests of progress.

Keller House, c.1895. 1217 Cobb. A vernacular approximation of the Stick style.

J. W. Hamilton House, 759 SE Kane. A large Queen Anne House with free classic elements. It was built for James Watson Hamilton, a circuit judge.

Napoleon Rice House, c.1893. 709 SE Kane. A corner-towered Queen Anne house that has been recycled for commercial use. It was once the home of businessman and local politician Napoleon Rice.

Parrot House, c.1891. 1772 SE Jackson. Queen Anne with an unusual octagonal tower. It was built for an early resident of Roseburg, Moses Parrot, a shoemaker from Wales.

Jacob Kamm House, Portland, 1871

J.M. Bunn House, Yamhill, 1888

Salem

The city was laid out in 1846 by New England missionaries who had arrived in the Willamette Valley a decade earlier hoping to convert the Indians. Swelled by American settlers, the new town was soon thriving as an agricultural center and by 1851 had replaced Oregon City as the capital of the territory. Today it retains some interesting relics from its nineteenth-century past, including the home of one of its founders, Jason Lee. An area of town that may also be of interest is the *Court-Chemeketa Historic District*, where homes dating as far back as the 1870s can be found. Its rough boundaries are Chemeketa and Court Streets between 14th and 18th.

Port House, *Deepwood,* 1895. 1116 Mission SE. Architect: W. C. Knighton. A large Queen Anne house built by Dr. Luke Port. Knighton who served as the Oregon State Architect also designed the state *Supreme Court Building. Deepwood* is now operated as a municipal museum open to the public. **503 363-1825.**

• **Asahel Bush House,** 1878. 600 Mission SE. Italianate. Originally the home of pioneering banker and newspaper publisher, Asahel Bush, it is now a municipal museum open to the public. *p. 32.*

Jason Lee House, 1841. 260 12th in Mission Mill Village. Jason Lee, Salem's founder and the first Christian missionary to work in the Willamette Valley, built this two-and-a-half story rectangular house, one of the oldest in Oregon. It has been moved from its original location to Mission Mill Village, a complex that shelters several other historical structures. **503 585-7012.**

David McCully House, 1865. 1365 John St. S. Carpenter's Gothic with a symmetrical front and a central gable with double pointed-arch windows.

Sauvie Island

Bybee-Howell House, 1856. 13901 NW Howell Park Rd. A large Greek Revival house built by Col. James F. Bybee, a horse breeder. It was later purchased by Dr. Benjamin Howell, another early settler. It is now the centerpiece of Howell Territorial Park, which is maintained by Multnomah County and is open for tours. Sauvie Island is located northwest of Portland where the Willamette joins the Columbia. **503 621-3344.**

The Dalles

The Dalles got its name from the French fur trappers who frequented the upper Columbia in the early nineteenth century. Later, in the 1840s, it became important as the site where the Oregon trail met the Columbia River. In the decade that followed, it expanded again when the army enlarged Fort Dalles in response to the Yakima Indian War of 1855. The town enjoyed modest prosperity throughout the rest of the century and has retained a nice assortment of houses and churches from that period. But its crown jewel is the *Surgeon's Quarters,* which must rank as one of the most important surviving examples of Gothic Revival domestic architecture in the United States.

• **Fort Dalles Surgeon's Quarters,** 1856. 1500 Garrison at 15th. Architect: Louis Scholl. A textbook example of Rural Gothic styling drawn directly from A. J. Downing's *Architecture of Country Houses.* As in the case of Fort Simcoe's *Commanding Officer's Quarters,* Alexander Jackson Davis may also have contributed to this design. The *Surgeon's Quarters* is now a museum. *p. 6.*

Queen Anne House, c. 1895. SW corner 9th and Union. Quaint, towered, and bespindled.

Gothic Revival House, c.1875. 413 W. 3rd. A center-gabled Gothic survival.

• **Thompson House,** c.1890. North side of 3rd, between Lincoln and Liberty. John L. Thompson was a blacksmith from Boston. *p. 49.*

Williams House, c.1899. 608 W. 6th. A large, towered Queen Anne, bespindled with a wraparound porch. It is, no doubt, the fanciest Victorian in town.

St. Peter's Church, 1898. Third and Lincoln. Gothic Revival in brick with Carrara marble, Povey stained glass and a lofty spire. It is available for tours by the public. **541 296-5686.**

Union

This eastern Oregon town of about two thousand was founded in 1878 and has a number of interesting Victorian homes, all privately owned. The even smaller town of Cove, not far away, is also worth a visit.

Mendel C. Israel House "Wildwood," c.1869. Main and Bryon. An expansive and extraordinary villa-style house, mostly Gothic Revival, but with some Italianate elements as well.

• **Abel Eaton House,** c.1898. 464 N. Main. A large, brick dwelling with a host of eclectic details: mansard roof, classical porch posts, Palladian windows, Queen Anne cresting, and bulls-eye tower dormers. *p. 43.*

Queen Anne House, 1884. 5th and Elm. A large, sumptuously decorated Queen Anne residence.

West Linn

Lewthwaite-Moffatt House, 1896. 4891 Willamette Falls Dr. A rambling Queen Anne residence with a corner turret. West Linn is located across the river from Oregon City.

Weston

Isham Saling House, 1880. Water St. An almost square brick house with round headed windows and an Italianate loggia across the front. It is interesting in comparison to the Dowell House in Jacksonville. Weston is located in Umatilla County, northeast of Pendleton on Route 11.

Wolf Creek

Wolf Creek Tavern, c.1870. Twenty miles north of Grants Pass, off I-5. The tavern opened in the early 1870s as a stage-coach stop and has been in nearly continuous operation ever since. A two-story Classical Revival structure, it has been restored and refurbished with period decorations and furniture.

Woodburn

Settlemier House, 1889. 355 N. Settlemier Ave. The Queen Anne residence of Jesse Settlemier, a pioneering nurseryman who founded Woodburn and served as its first mayor. Now a house museum maintained by the French Prairie Historical Society, it is available for group tours by appointment. **503 982-1897.** Woodburn is located off I-5 between Portland and Salem.

Yamhill

This small town in Oregon's Wine Country southwest of Portland features two high-style houses of remarkable quality.

• **J. M. Bunn House,** c.1888. 285 SW 3rd. The French Second Empire home of John Marion Bunn, an important figure in the early history of Yamhill. His granddaughter, Beverly Bunn Cleary, a children's author, made the house the setting for her book *Emily's Runaway Imagination. p. 39.*

• **Laughlin House,** 1879. 100 Laurel. Gothic with Italianate elements. This stylish residence originally belonged to Lee Laughlin, a pioneer homesteader who later became a state senator. *p. 17.*

Zylstra House, Coupeville, 1889

Bartlett House, Port Townsend, 1883

French Cottage, Fort Vancouver, c.1880

Capt. Sawyer House, Port Townsend, 1887

Abel Eaton House, Union, c.1898

Washington

As in Oregon, most of Washington's earliest surviving architecture is located in the western third of the state. From the Hudson's Bay outpost of Fort Vancouver on the Columbia River, pioneers moved north to the Tumwater Falls area and then along the shores of Puget Sound. With the coming of the railroad in the 1870s and 1880s Bellingham, Everett, Seattle, Tacoma, and Port Townsend all joined in the competition to become the terminus of one of the branches. As often happens in such contests, the winners lost most of their early architecture while the losers—Port Townsend most spectacularly—retained much of theirs.

In the eastern two-thirds of the state, early development was slowed by several notorious Indian massacres. Later in the century the Idaho gold rush and the arrival of the railroad turned Spokane into the fastest growing city in the northwest.

Bellingham

Bellingham was formed from the union of four distinct communities: Bellingham, Fairhaven, Whatcom and New Whatcom, formerly Sehome. Henry Roeder, the earliest white settler in the area, arrived in 1852. Others soon followed, attracted by the lumber, fishing, furs, and coal that the area had to offer.

At the end of the 1880s rumors that Fairhaven was to become the terminus of the Great Northern Railroad fueled a building boom and an orgy of speculation. Unfortunately for local boosters, that plum went to Everett. As a result Bellingham, like Port Townsend was left with an architectural legacy that includes quite a number of Victorian houses and late nineteenth-century commercial buildings.

Whatcom

Located northwest of downtown Bellingham, this area, the oldest in town, harbors a number of houses dating from the 1880s and '90s.

• **Keyes House,** 1892. 2230 Henry. Architect: D. B. Provoost. This gabled-ell suburban cottage was built by Philip Isensee, but bears the name of a long-time resident, Dr. William Keyes. The style is High Victorian Italianate, and the plan—the same used in the *Ferguson House* in Astoria—was taken from *Bicknell's Detail,*

Cottage and Constructive Architecture (1872). *p. 34.*

• **Schram House,** 1895. 2601 West. The work of a carpenter-builder, this Free Classic Queen Anne house displays a number of elements derived from the Classical Revival movement. *p. 65.*

• **Shields House,** 1900. 2215 Utter. The Eastlake-detailed Queen Anne residence of *fin de siecle* lumberman Robert Shields. The classical columns on the porch are transitional to the new Classical Revival style. *p. 65.*

Loggie House, 1885. 2203 Utter. An Eastlake villa.

New Whatcom

The settlement once known as Sehome and later New Whatcom now comprises downtown Bellingham.

Museum of History and Art, 1892. 121 Prospect St. Architect: Alfred Lee. Formerly the New Whatcom City Hall, this striking, mansard-roofed civic building was restored and refurbished in the wake of a devestating 1962 fire.

Morse House, 1896. 1014 N. Garden. Architect: Alfred Lee. A corner-towered Queen Anne villa with Eastlake details. Now the *North Garden Inn.*

Fairhaven

The Fairhaven Historic District, located south of downtown Bellingham, is roughly bounded by 10th and 13th Streets and Columbia and Larrabee Avenues. Besides some interesting houses, it boasts a dozen or so brick commercial buildings from its boom years in the late 1880s and 90s. The bricks, incidentally, arrived as ballast on incoming lumber ships.

• **Wardner's Castle,** 1890. 1103 15th and Knox. Architect: Kirtland Cutter. Entrepreneur James Wardner built this sixteen-room mansion after making a killing in Fairhaven real estate. It shows the clear influence of the fashionable Shingle style. It is now *The Castle Bed & Breakfast.* **360 676-0974.** *p. 69.*

• **Gamwell House,** 1892. 1001 16th. Architects: Longstaff and Black. The elaborate and eclectic home of Roland G. Gamwell, an engineer who helped plan Tacoma's interurban rail system. It was designed by a pair of architects from Boston. *p. 64.*

Bateman House, 1891. 1034 15th. A hefty Queen Anne residence with a broad square tower capped with a concave mansard roof.

Larrabee House, 1891. 1131 15th. An "L"-shaped house decorated with cut-out decoration in the gables.

Bothell

W. A. Hannan House. 10222 Main. A two-story house in the Gothic Revival style. Built by pioneer merchant William Hannan, it has been relocated from its original location and now serves as a house museum. It is maintained by the Bothell Historical Museum Society, which also sponsors the nearby Beckstrom Log Cabin. **425 486-1889.** Bothell is located a few miles northeast of Seattle at the junction of I-405 and Hwy. 9.

Chinook Vicinity

Across the Columbia River from Astoria, a number of late nineteenth-century architectural attractions can be found. The town of Chinook has a small collection of vernacular houses from that period, as well as *St. Mary's Church*–a wooden, Gothic Revival structure located on the highway outside of town. Nearby is *Fort Columbia State Park* which features several well-preserved military houses dating from around 1900. To the west, near Ilwaco are two picturesque lighthouses, *Cape Disappointment Light* (1856) and *North Head Light* (1898) and another former military installation, *Fort Canby.* To the east along Route 4 is the *Grays River Covered Bridge* and the rustic hamlet of Skamokawa.

Colfax

James A. Perkins House, 1880. 623 N. Perkins. A country house styled as an Italianate villa. Originally the home of one of the town founders, it is now the headquarters of the Whitman County Historical Society. Colfax, the oldest town in the Palouse is located on U.S. 195 about sixty miles south of Spokane. The downtown area also features several nineteenth-century commercial buildings.

Coupeville

Coupeville, on Whidbey Island, dates from 1852 when it was established by Captain Thomas Coupe as a harbor for sailing vessels. Although never very large, the community contains a capsule history of Victorian house styles, ranging from the Gothic Revival through the Queen Anne. The Central Whidbey Island Historic District is a unique reserve administered by the National Park Service. It extends roughly six miles on either side of Coupeville. The island is located north of Seattle across the Admiralty Inlet from Port Townsend.

• **James Zylstra House,** 1889. 7th and Center. Builder: H. B. Lovejoy. As signaled by the jaunty, concave mansard roof, this is an example of the French cottage style. Lovejoy, Coupeville's leading carpitect, built it as his own residence. *p. 42.*

Methodist Church, 1883. 9th and Center. Mostly Gothic Revival with some Queen Anne touches.

• **Joseph B. Libbey House,** 1870. Main at 4th. A sober, center-gabled Gothic Revival cottage. *p. 14.*

• **Kineth House,** 1887. 7th and N. Main. A bracketed Italianate house built for John and Jane Kineth. Now a bed and breakfast. **1 800 688-2683.** *p. 25.*

• **Jacob Jenne House,** c.1889. 602 N. Main. The Italianate home of Jacob Jenne, a German immigrant who ran the Central Hotel in Coupeville. It is now a bed and breakfast. **360 678-5305.** *p. 25.*

• **Will Jenne House,** 1890. 508 S. Main. Let's call it Queen Anne, though the overall configuration and roof forms are more characteristic of the Stick style. *p. 49.*

Davenport

The seat of Lincoln County, Davenport is located about thirty miles west of Spokane on U. S. Hwy. 2.

Lincoln County Courthouse, 1897. 450 Logan. Classical Revival.

Hoople House, 1886. 308 Logan. Queen Anne.

McInnis House, 1889. 1001 Morgan. Queen Anne.

Hochstedler House, Albany, c.1889

Benjamin Young House, Astoria, 1888

Skipton House, Albany, c.1895

John Ralston House, Albany, 1889

Dayton

This eastern Washington town, located north of Waitsburg on U. S. 12, retains a number of interesting Victorian structures.

Dayton Railroad Depot, 1881. 2nd and Commercial Streets. This Stick-style railroad station, the oldest in the state, was built by the Oregon Railroad and Navigation Company. It is now a railroad museum.

Columbia County Courthouse, 1886. 341 E. Main. A fine, brick and stucco courthouse in the Italianate style complete with belvedere.

Dr. Pietrzycki House, c.1882. 415 East Clay. An eclectic, late Victorian residence with a jerkinhead gable, Italianate brackets and wooden quoins at the corners. Originally the residence of a physician and philanthropist, it is now the *Purple House Bed and Breakfast.* **509 382-3159.**

Queen Anne House, c.1890. 2nd at Spring. Queen Anne.

Ellensburg

Located on the east side of the Cascades near the center of the state, Ellensburg is the seat of Kittitas County and the home of Central Washington University. Founded in the early 1870s, it became something of a boom town when the railroad came through in 1886. But as in Seattle and Spokane a disastrous fire in 1889 destroyed most of its early architecture. The Ellensburg Historic District, which includes twenty historical buildings, is bounded by 3rd and 6th Avenues, Main and Ruby Streets.

Washington State Normal School Building *(Barge Hall),* 1893. Eighth Ave. Architect: E. C. Price. A two-and-a-half story building— the oldest on the Central Washington State campus—in the High Victorian Gothic style.

Davidson Block, 1889. Pearl and Fourth. A handsome block of store buildings with segmental-arched windows and a corner tower.

Ferndale

• **Hovander House,** 1903. 5299 Neilson Rd. Architect: Håkan Olsson Hovander. Hovander, a Swedish architect, designed his retirement home, in a Gothic style reminiscent of his homeland. The farm is now a county park. **360 384-3444.** Ferndale is located a few miles north of Bellingham. *p. 14.*

Fort Simcoe

Fort Simcoe was constructed in response to the Indian uprising of 1855, and was later turned over to the Department of Indian Affairs. In the last half of the twentieth century it was acquired by the state of Washington and has since become an historic park. With its well-maintained buildings and unspoiled parade ground, it offers a very good picture of a mid-nineteenth century frontier army post. The fort is located southeast of Yakima, about thirty miles west of Toppenish on Route 220. **509 874-2372.**

• **Commanding Officer's Quarters,** c.1857. 5150 Fort Simcoe Rd. White Swan. Architect: Louis Scholl. A textbook example of a Carpenters Gothic cottage and a rare example of "Picturesque" military architecture. Designed by the same draftsman who did the *Fort Dalles Surgeon's Quarters,* it is based on "A Villa Farm-house in the Bracketed Style," which was featured in A. J. Downing's *Architecture of Country Houses.* Since the illustration in that volume bears the signature "Anderson," a favorite engraver of Alexander Jackson Davis, we may assume that the foremost house architect of the period also had a hand in creating the design. *p. 7.*

Goldendale

The seat of Klickitat County in south central Washington, Goldendale is located north of the Columbia River at the junction of U. S. 97 and Route 142.

Presby House, 1902. 127 W. Broadway. Queen Anne with an unusual, central tower. It was built by Winthrop Bartlett Presby who served as a U. S. Land Commissioner and Washington State Senator. It is now a museum run by the Klickitat Historical Society. **509 773-4303.**

Sleeper House, c.1885. 203 W. Broadway. Italianate with a pent roof and brackets.

House, 1880. 210 E. Court. A large, boxy house with fancy gable trim and Eastlake fancywork.

Holmes House, Astoria, 1890

Will Jenne House, Coupeville, 1890

Huntley House, Oregon City, 1896

Thompson House, The Dalles, c.1890

Chambers House, Eugene, c.1895

Gray-Hackett House, Oregon City, 1894

Starrett House, Port Townsend, 1889

W.G. White House, Olympia, 1893

Edward Howell House, Oregon City, c.1885

Wilson House, Corvallis, 1891

Peter Mutty House, Port Townsend, 1891

51

Goldsmith House, Portland, 1896

Gerson House, Port Townsend, 1889

C.D. Drain House, Drain, c.1891

Jeremiah Nunan House, Jacksonville, c.1892

Goeller House, Klamath Falls, c.1905

Sullivan House, La Connor, 1892

Hassard House, Drain, c.1900

Sherwood House, Coquille, 1901

55

Fotheringham House, Spokane, 1897

L. C. Marshall House, Albany, c.1895

Gaches Mansion, La Connor, 1891

Heceta House, Heceta Head, 1894

Poulson House, Portland, 1895

Ison House, Baker City, 1887

Hidden House, Vancouver, 1885

F.W. James House, Port Townsend, 1891

John Palmer House, Portland, 1890

Queen Anne House, Seattle, c.1889

Ulysses S. Grant House, Fort Vancouver, c.1885

Shelton-McMurphey-Johnson House, Eugene, 1888

Gamwell House, Bellingham, 1892

Schram House, Bellingham, 1895

Shields House, Bellingham, 1900

Ben Olsen House, Vader, c.1905

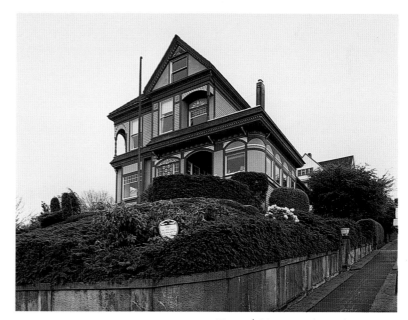

Foard House, Astoria, 1892

Hoquiam

Although it was settled in 1859, Hoquiam did not begin to assume importance as a lumber center until the 1880s. From that time until well into the twentieth century its domestic architecture was dominated by a succession of lumbermen's mansions. One of them the Colonial Revival **Polson House** (1923) has become a museum devoted to the early history of the Grays Harbor area.

• **Lytle House, "Hoquiam's Castle,"** 1897. 515 Chenault. The palatial residence of lumberman Robert F. Lytle. The style is High Victorian Eclectic with traces of the Shingle and Romanesque. It is available for public tours. **360 533-2005**. *p. 77.*

Lytle House, 509 Chenault. The Queen Anne residence of Robert Lytle's brother, another lumberman. Now a bed and breakfast.

La Connor

First settled in 1868, this Skagit Valley town south of Bellingham was originally called "Swinomish" after a local Indian tribe. However, John Connor, one of its first settlers, renamed the town in honor of his wife, Louise A. Connor. Now a fishing port and artists' colony, it has a flavor of genteel rusticity. The Skagit-La Connor Historic District, bounded by 2nd and the Snohomish Canal, comprises mostly waterfront commercial buildings and several interesting houses.

• **Gaches Mansion,** 1891. 702 S. 2nd. A large Queen Anne with traces of the Stick style and Elizabethan half timbering. Built by English émigré George Gaches, it has been restored and is available for tours and rentals. **360 466-4288**. *p. 58.*

Magnus Anderson Cabin, 1869. 2nd and Morris. The residence of one of the earliest settlers in the area.

• **Sullivan House,** 1892. 1624 La Connor Whitney Rd. This Queen Anne farmhouse was built by Michael Sullivan, one of the first farmers in the Skagit Valley to dike and dam the marshes near La Connor. Built of cedar from Camano Island, it appears to have been based on design No. 21 in G. F. Barber's *Cottage Souvenir No. 2.* *p. 55.*

White Swan Guest House, c.1898. 1388 Moore Rd, on Fir Island SE of La Connor. A farmhouse embellished with Victorian trappings. Now a bed and breakfast. **360 445-6805.**

Medical Lake

"Lac de Medicine," as it was originally called, was founded by a French Canadian, Andrew Lefevre, who discovered the curative powers of the local waters. It is located about twenty miles southwest of Spokane.

Hallett House, 1900-03. 623 Lake. The eccentric and eclectic mansion of Lord Stanley Hallett, an Englishman who helped develop the town of Medical Lake. It is known locally as "The Castle."

Community Church, 1889. NW corner Ladd and Washington. Gothic Revival.

Olympia-Tumwater

The settlement that became Tumwater dates from 1845 when the first pioneers arrived from Fort Vancouver and established a settlement on the banks of the Deschutes River. Within a few years, a number of saw mills were taking advantage of power supplied by the Tumwater Falls. By the end of the nineteenth century the local artesian wells had attracted the attention of several brewers. Meanwhile, in 1853, neighboring Olympia had become the capital of the new Washington Territory. Today some remnants of the area's oldest architecture remains, but much was lost during the construction of Interstate 5 in the late 1950s.

• **William G. White House,** 1893. 1431 11th Ave SE. Queen Anne with a square corner-tower and elaborate Eastlake gable trusses. *p. 50.*

Patnude House, 1893. 1234 8th SE. Charles Patnude, a local builder, constructed his own home in the Rural Gothic style.

Bigelow House, c.1860. 918 Glass NE. Gothic Revival. It's first owner was Daniel Bigelow, lawyer, legislator and one of the first to advocate that Washington separate from the rest of the Oregon Territory. Purchased and restored by the Bigelow House Preservation Association in the mid 1990s, the house is now available for public tours. **360 753-1215.**

Tumwater Historic District

The district is roughly bounded by I-5, Capitol Way, and Capitol Lake.

• **Crosby House,** c.1858. 708 Deschutes Way. A vernacular cottage with Greek and Gothic Revival elements. It was once the home of pioneers Nathaniel and Cordelia Crosby, Bing Crosby's grandparents. It is now maintained by the city of Tumwater and the Daughters of the Pioneers of Washington. *p. 10.*

Henderson House, 1905. 602 N. Deschutes Way. A two-story structure with a Queen Anne corner tower. Now a museum devoted to pioneer life in the Deschutes River area. **206 753 8583.**

Oysterville

Oysterville owes its name and early success to a small, flavorful shellfish that bred prodigiously in the protected waters of the Willapa Bay, north of the mouth of the Columbia. Robert Espy and Isaac Clark, the first white settlers to take advantage of this bounty, built a log house in the early 1850s and watched as a town grew up around them. The community thrived for a quarter century or so before drifting into quiet dormancy. The community is the subject of a wonderfully droll memoir, *Oysterville*, by W. R. Espy, grandson of one of the founders. The Oysterville Historic District was created in 1976.

• **Tom Crellin House,** 1869. Territory Rd. at Clay. A two-story, cross-gabled house with Gothic Revival decorative elements. It originally belonged to Tom Crellin, an oysterman from the Isle of Man. *p. 14.*

Oysterville Church, 1892. Territory Rd at Clay. A simple, cross-gabled structure with a Queen Anne tower-belfry.

R. H. Espy House, 1871. Territory Rd at Division. The home that one of Oysterville's founders built for his bride when he got married. As a batchelor, he had been content with the log cabin he occupied for nearly twenty years.

Port Gamble

Founded in 1853 by three lumbermen—A. J. Pope, William Talbot, and Cyrus Walker—Port Gamble is like a New England village transported to Puget Sound. Still owned by Pope and Talbot, it is said to have been inspired by East Machias, Maine, the founders' hometown.

Although the mill closed in 1996, more than two dozen restored and Victorian-era homes and buildings remain. These include some interesting vernacular Gothic and Italianate cottages and a perfect copy of a New England church. The area has been granted historical status by the National Register of Historic Places. *p. 14.*

Walker-Ames House, 1889. Rainier Ave. A Queen Anne house built for the resident manager of the Pope and Talbot Sawmill.

Jackson House, 1871. 10 Rainier Ave.

St. Paul's Episcopal Church, 1870. Rainier Ave. A fine Gothic Revival church modeled, it is said, on the Congregational Church in East Machias, Maine.

Port Townsend

Port Townsend, one of the premier sites of surviving Victoriana in the Pacific Northwest, was founded in 1851 by a group of settlers from Portland. Because of its strategic location at the entrance to Puget Sound, it enjoyed immediate success and soon joined other Washington cities in the scramble to become the northwest terminus of the intercontinental railroad. In the 1880s it experienced a series of speculative building booms based on a local railroad scheme that ultimately came to naught. When the bubble burst in 1890, further development in Port Townsend ceased and most of its population departed. As a result, much of the architecture built during its peak years is still standing today.

Just outside of town is the *Point Wilson Lighthouse* (1914) and *Fort Worden*, which was established in 1886 for coastal defense. Now a Washington State Park, it retains an interesting selection of turn-of-the-century military housing, mostly Georgian in style. **360 385-4730.**

James and Hasting Building, 1889. NE Water and Tyler. Architect: Fisher and Clark. A commercial building that seems to have been inspired by Venetian Gothic models.

N.D. Hill Building, 1889. SE Water and Quincy. Architect: Elmer Fisher. A three-story commercial block with Italianate leanings.

J. W. Griffiths House, c.1889. 2030 Monroe. An end-gabled house similar in plan and some ornamental details to the Harper and Stockand Houses.

J.C. Saunders House, Port Townsend, 1891

Wardner House, Bellingham, 1890

James Stockand House, 1887. 110 F. Builders: Peter and James Stockand. Basically Queen Anne with some fine Eastlake touches. It was originally the home of local merchant James W. Stockand and his wife, Julie Kineth of Whidbey Island. The house was restored in the 1970s.

F.C. Harper House, 1889. 502 Reed. A fairly ordinary facade has been enlivened by carved brackets on the front bay and subtle Eastlake details in the gable boards. This house is thought to have been built by one of Port Townsend's many realtors.

Henry Landes House, 1871-82. 1034 Franklin. In 1882 Landes, a "Kentucky Colonel" and state senator, added the Queen Anne elements on the left side of the facade to a classical Revival house that had been built in 1871.

Milo P. Ward House, 1889. 1707 Jackson St. A speculative house built by one of Port Townsend's many realtors. Recent owners have received the Mary P. Johnson Award for their restoration efforts.

• **Peter Mutty House,** 1891. 640 Taylor at Lawrence. An Eastlake-Queen Anne cottage with gilt trim and iron roof cresting. *p. 51.*

• **Frank Bartlett House,** 1883. 314 Polk. A two-story frame house with a distinctive concave mansard roof. It was originally the residence of Frank Bartlett, a young entrepreneur who came to Port Townsend seeking his fortune. *p. 42.*

• **Capt. Charles Sawyer House,** 1887. Polk at Jefferson. Less formal than the Bartlett house next door, this French Cottage has a jauntily curved mansard roof—and a superb view of Port Townsend and the Admiralty Inlet. *p. 42.*

Capt Enoch S. Fowler House, c.1865. Polk at Washington. The oldest frame house in Port Townsend. Fowler was a local builder and the captain of the mail boat.

St. Paul's Episcopal Church, 1865. Jefferson and Tyler. Builder: A. Horace Tucker. A beautifully proportioned—and preserved—Gothic Revival church. On at least two occasions, according to legend, the church bell alerted fog-bound ships, saving them from disaster.

Jefferson County Courthouse, 1892. Jefferson and Cass. Architect: William A. Ritchie. This classic nineteenth-century courthouse, one of the oldest in Washington, displays elements of both the Chateauesque and Richardsonian Romanesque styles.

• **Starrett House,** 1889. 744 Clay. The unique creation of builder George Starrett. Famous for its spiral tower staircase and allegorical ceiling fresco, the house now serves as a bed and breakfast. **360 385-3205.** *p. 50.*

• **F. W. James House,** 1891. 1238 Washington. The Queen Anne residence of Englishman, F. W. James, a customs agent and self-described "capitalist." It is now a bed and breakfast. **360 385-1238.** *p. 61.*

• **Gerson House,** 1889. 1427 Washington. A gabled-ell suburban townhouse with Queen Anne and Eastlake decorative elements. *p. 52.*

Downs House, 1886. Filmore and Clay. Italianate. It was originally the home of a Port Townsend sawmill operator.

Charles Pink House, 1868. Lawrence and Harrison. Architect: Horace Tucker. Newly restored after years of neglect, the house is an example of the Greek Revival style—with alterations and additions.

Adams House, 1887. 1028 Tyler at F. A large, three-story Queen Anne house with a properly scaled tower to match. It was built by Albert Adams, a builder speculator, for his father, John Quincy Adams, a descendant of the president. It is now a bed and breakfast. **360 379-8832.**

Rothschild House, 1868. Washington and Taylor. The Greek Revival home of D. C. H. Rothschild. It has been restored and is maintained as a museum open to the public by the Washington State Parks system.

• **Hastings House,** 1890. 313 Walker. A corner-towered Queen Anne built by speculator Frank Hastings just as Port Townsend's boom was going bust. It later served briefly as the office of a German consular official, hence its other name, "The Old German Consulate." It is now a bed and breakfast. **360-385-6753.** *Back cover.*

• **J. C. Saunders House,** 1891. Sims Way off Hwy. 20. Architect: Edward A. Batwell. A large and sophisticated Queen Anne house with overtones of the toney Shingle style. It was originally the home of real-estate speculator Saunders. *p. 68.*

• **Eisenbeis House,** *Manresa Hall,* 1892. 7th and Sheridan. The Chateauesque home of Charles Eisenbeis, a German baker who became Port Townsend's first mayor. It is now an inn. **360 385-5750.** *p. 76.*

Puyallup

Ezra Meeker Mansion, 1890, 312 Spring Street off Hwy 512. Architects: Farrell and Darmer. The elaborate High Victorian Italianate home of Ezra Meeker, pioneer, hops farmer, town founder, and Oregon Trail publicist. Now a house museum, it is open for tours. **253 848-1770.** Puyallup is located southeast of Tacoma.

Ritzville

Dr. Frank E. Burroughs House, 1889-1902. 408 Main. A large, turn-of-the-century house with free classic elements. It is now a museum devoted to the life of a country doctor. Ritzville is located on I-90 about halfway between Ellensburg and Spokane.

Seattle

Thanks to rapid growth and urbanization in the twentieth century, Victorian buildings have become a rare and endangered species in Seattle. Now the largest city in the Northwest, the early town showed little promise of the regional dominance it was to achieve. It was founded in 1852, but its population hovered below a thousand for the next twenty years. Port Townsend rivaled it as a shipping point, and Tacoma won out in the competition to become the terminus of the Northern Pacific Railroad. To add injury to insult, a devastating fire destroyed much of the downtown area in 1889. This disaster accompanied and actually spurred new growth—the city's population soared to 35,000 in 1890—but the reconstruction favored civic and commercial buildings and displaced housing to the nearer suburbs. When even more rapid expansion overtook twentieth-century Seattle, these new neighborhoods also fell to redevelopment.

Stimson-Green Mansion, 1901. 1204 Minor Ave. Architect: Kirtland Cutter. The half-timbered Tudor residence of lumberman C.D. Stimson. The house is open for group tours by appointment.

• **Queen Anne House,** c.1889. 520 W. Kinnear. One of the last Victorian survivors in the Queen Anne Hill section of Seattle. *p. 61.*

• **Ward House,** 1882. 520 E. Denny Way. A rare Victorian survivor in Seattle, this Italianate house had to be relocated to save it from destruction. It serves today as an office building. *p. 28.*

Skamokawa

Located in Wahkiakum County on the lower Columbia, Skamokawa became a National Historic District in 1976. It preserves a number of turn-of-the-century vernacular houses and the c.1880s *Redmen Lodge.* Nearby, outside of Grays River, is the unusual *Grays River Covered Bridge.*

Snohomish

Southeast of Everett on Route 2, Snohomish was founded in 1859, and has managed to retain a number of Victorian houses and commercial buildings. The Snohomish Historic District is roughly bounded by Ave. E, 5th St., Union Ave., the Northern Pacific RR, and the Snohomish River.

Queen Anne House, 1887. 223 Ave. A. This Queen Anne residence has a shingle-clad, centrally-placed tower, faux quoins, and an explosion of cut-out ornament in the front gable.

Spokane

The area around Spokane was founded as an outpost of the Northwest Fur Company soon after the Lewis and Clark expedition of 1805-06. But the city did not attain a true civic identity until the 1870s. In the decade that followed, the Northern Pacific Railroad and a gold rush in the Idaho panhandle conspired to make it a regional center. As in Seattle, a fire in 1889 destroyed much of the town's early Victorian architecture. Today most of what remains can be found in Brown's Addition, which developed, for the most part, after the conflagration. This fashionable residential neighborhood west of the downtown area owes much of its best architecture to Kirtland Kelsey Cutter whose career began there. Also noteworthy is the Cathedral of St. John, a splendid Gothic structure located downtown at 12th and Grand.

Campbell House, 1898. West 2316 1st. Architect: Kirtland Cutter. A large half-timbered Tudor-style house designed for Amasa B. Campbell, who made a fortune in the gold fields of Idaho and British Columbia. Donated to the Eastern Washington Historical Society, it has been restored and is open for tours. **509 456 3931.**

Jones House, 1890. West 2022 1st. Queen Anne.

Flippin House, Clatskanie, 1899

MacKenzie House, Portland, 1894

Queen Anne House, c.1895. West 2003 1st. A corner-towered Queen Anne.

Queen Anne House, West 1923 1st. Architect: W. J. Carpenter.

Luhn House, c.1889. West 2236 Pacific. Architects: Cutter and Malgren.

• **Patrick F. Clark Mansion,** 1898. West 2208 2nd. Architect: Kirtland Cutter. An eclectic, *fin de siecle,* brick and sandstone mansion designed for Patrick "Patsy" Clark, an Irish immigrant who made his fortune in mining. It is now *Patsy Clark's Mansion,* an upscale restaurant. **509 838-8300.** *p. 80.*

• **Fotheringham House,** c.1897. West 2128 2nd. A nicely restored and preserved corner-towered Queen Anne that belonged to Spokane's first mayor. Now a bed and breakfast. **509 838-1891.** *p. 56.*

Stimmel House, 1889. West 2421 2nd. A well-preserved Queen Anne residence.

House, West 1905 Pacific. A quiet and reserved representative of the Queen Anne style.

Colonial Apartments, 1890. West 2020-30 Riverside. This group is a rarity in the Northwest—a row of attached houses in the Queen Anne style.

House, 1920 Riverside. A small residence with particularly lacy spandrels.

House, c.1898. 2019 Riverside. Queen Anne in transition to shingled Colonial Revival.

Sprague

Church of Mary Queen of Heaven, 1902. A large Gothic Revival church in brick. Sprague is located on I-90 about 30 miles southwest of Spokane.

Steilacoom

One of the oldest towns in the state, Steilacoom was founded in the early 1850s. Now a designated historic district, it is situated on the south shore of Puget Sound near Puyallup, and preserves a number of early, mostly vernacular, residences in the Steilacoom Historic District located between Nisqually Street and Puget Sound.

Orr House, 1857. 1811 Rainier. A two-story frame house with Greek Revival elements. Open for public tours.

Davidson House, 1858. 1802 Commercial.

Tacoma

Founded in the early 1850s, Tacoma started off as just another lumber port on Puget Sound. However, in 1873 it won the fierce northwest intercity railroad competition when it was selected as the Northern Pacific terminus. For a time, Tacoma was the most promising city on the sound, with an expanding population and fine residential neighborhoods. However, beginning in the 1890s, it began to lose out to Seattle as it became a gritty industrial and port city. In the twentieth century, development—read sprawl—tended to flatten most of the city's nineteenth-century domestic architecture.

Geiger House, 1889. 912 North I St. A nicely restored Queen Anne residence with Stick and Eastlake decoration.

Murray House, c.1905. 402 N. Sheridan. An unusual combination of Gothic and Colonial Revival elements—an extremely steep-pitched roof, with radically elongated dormers to match, and thick classical columns on the front veranda.

Union Station, 1911. 1717 Pacific. Architects: Reed and Stern. An opulent, Neo-Baroque railroad depot with a copper-plated dome. Renovated in recent years, it has been recycled for commercial use.

Old City Hall, 1893. 7th between Commerce and Pacific. Architect: Hatherton and McIntosh. A five-story stone civic building. Italianate with Florentine influences.

St. Peter's Episcopal, 1873. Starr Between 29th and 30th. A board-and-batten Gothic Revival church, but with twentieth-century alterations and additions.

Vader

• **Ben Olsen House,** 1905-13. South end of D St. A late-blooming Queen Anne house that has been recently restored. Vader is located a few miles west of I-5 between Longview and Chehalis. *p. 65.*

Vancouver

The oldest city in Washington was originally founded as Fort Vancouver in 1824. It began as a Hudson's Bay Company outpost, and later became a U. S. Army fort. Today the town retains a few scattered houses from its Victorian period as well as a prize assortment of late nineteenth-century military buildings at *Fort Vancouver National Historic Site*.

• **Officers' Row**, 611-1616 E. Evergreen Blvd. A parade of twenty-one frame structures, including ten houses and eleven duplexes in a variety of styles ranging from southern plantationesque to Queen Anne.

• **Marshall House**, 1886. 1301 Officers Row. A large, corner-towered Queen Anne villa, handsome but restrained. It takes its name from its most famous occupant, General George Marshall, who masterminded American military strategy during World War II. ***Front Cover***

• **Ulysses S. Grant House**, 1849-1885. Officers Row. The original log house was covered with clapboard in the mid 1880s and remodeled to give it the look of a plantation of the old south. It is named for Ulysses S. Grant who spent a year at Fort Vancouver in the early 1850s. *p. 62.*

• **French Cottage**, c.1880. Officers Row. A small cottage with a mansard roof. *p. 42.*

• **L. M. Hidden House**, 1885. 100 W. 13th at Main. The Eastlake-style home of a prominent family who owned a brick works in Vancouver. It is now a restaurant. Another "Hidden" house, a Georgian-style brick residence, is at 110 W. 13th. *p. 60.*

Mansardic Cottage, 404 11th. A cottage with a mansard roof.

Dubois House, 902 Esther. A chaste Queen Anne dwelling.

Slocum House, 1867. 605 Esther St. An Italianate villa thought to have been modeled after a house in Rhode Island. Moved from its original site, it is now used by a local theater company.

Waitsburg

Bruce Memorial Museum, 1883. 318 Main. This Italianate mansion of one of the town founders has been restored by the Waitsburg Historical Society. **509-337-6287.** Waitsburg was laid out in 1868 by William Perry Bruce, a farmer and land developer. It is located between Walla Walla and Dayton on U. S. Hwy. 12.

Walla Walla

In response to the Whitman massacre of 1836 and the Indian uprising of 1855, a fort was established on the present site of Walla Walla, and the town grew up beside it. For the next few decades it prospered nicely as a regional center, but in the late 1880s it was eclipsed by its neighbor to the north, Spokane. For more than a century now, Walla Walla has managed to retain a good sampling of its nineteenth-century architecture. The *Whitman Mission*, which holds more historic than architectural interest, is located on U. S. Hwy. 12, seven miles west of town.

Kirkman House, 1880. 214 N. Colville. English-born cattle rancher William Kirkman built this fine, wood-trimmed, brick residence in the Italianate style. It is now a house museum. **509-529-4373.**

Michael Ward House, c.1876. 228 E. Poplar. A bracketed Italianate villa.

Queen Anne Villa, 1896. 208 S. Palouse. An enormous Queen Anne residence now in use as an apartment building.

County Courthouse, 1916. W. Main between 5th and 6th. Architects: Osterman and Siebert. Beaux Arts.

Downtown Commercial Buildings, East Main from 1st to 2nd Ave. This block displays a range of interesting store fronts, hotels and other buildings from the last quarter of the nineteenth century.

Eisenbeis House, Manresa Hall, Port Townsend, 1892

Piggot's Castle, Portland, 1892

Lytle House, "Hoquiam's Castle," Hoquiam, 1897

Select Bibliography

American Institute of Architects, Southwestern Oregon Chapter. *Style and Vernacular: A Guide to the Architecture of Lane County Oregon.* Eugene: Oregon Historical Society, 1983.

Andrews, Wayne. *American Gothic: Its Origins, Its Trials, Its Triumphs.* New York: Random House, 1975.

Barber, George F. *The Cottage Souvenir No. 2. A Repository of Artistic Cottage Architecture and Miscellaneous Designs.* Knoxville: S.B. Newman & Co., 1891. Reprint with Introduction by Michael A. Tomlan. Watkins Glen: American Life Foundation, 1982.

Bicknell, Amos Jackson. *Detail, Cottage, and Constructive Architecture.* New York: Bicknell & Co, 1873, 1881, 1886. Reprint. *Victorian Architecture: Two Pattern Books by A. J. Bicknell and William T. Comstock.* Introduction by John Maas. Watkins Glen: American Life Foundation, 1976.

Clark, Rosalind. *Oregon Style: Architecture 1840 to 1950s.* Portland: Professional Book Center, 1983.

Cleaveland, Henry, William Backus and Samuel Backus. *American Village Homes.* New York: D. Appleton & Co., 1856, 1869. Reprint. Watkins Glen: American Life Foundation, 1976.

Dennison, Allen T., and Wallace K. Huntington. *Victorian Architecture of Port Townsend, Washington.* Saanichton and Seattle: Hancock House, 1978.

De Wolfe, Fred. *Portland Tradition in Buildings and People.* Portland, OR: Press-22, 1980.

Downing, Andrew Jackson. *The Architecture of Country Houses.* D. Appleton & Co, 1850. Reprint. Introduction by J. Stewart Johnson. New York: Dover, 1969.

Foley, Mary Mix. *The American House.* New York: Harper & Row, 1980.

Gault, Vera Whitney. *Walking Tour of Astoria, Oregon.* By the author, 1393 Franklin Ave. 97103, 1978.

Gottfried, Herbert and Jan Jennings. *American Vernacular Design: 1870-1940.* New York: Van Nostrand Reinhold, 1985.

Hawkins, William John. *The Grand Era of Cast-Iron Architecture in Portland.* Portland: Binford & Mort, 1976.

Knuth, Priscilla. "'Picturesque' Frontier: The Army's Fort Dalles." *Oregon Historical Quarterly.* Dec 1966 and March 1967.

Maas, John. *The Gingerbread Age.* New York: Bramhall House, 1952.

McAlester, Virginia and Lee. *A Field Guide to American Houses.* New York: Alfred E. Knopf, 1985.

Matthews, Henry. *Kirtland Cutter: Architect in the Land of Promise.* Seattle: University of Washington Press, 1998

Schlereth, Thomas. *Victorian America: Transformations in Everyday Life, 1876-1915.* New York: Harper Collins, 1991.

Turbeville, Daniel. *A Catalog of Historic Bellingham Buildings: 1852-1915.* Bellingham: Municipal Arts Commission, 1977.

Woodbridge, Sally and Roger Montgomery. *A Guide to Architecture in Washington State.* Seattle: University of Washington Press, 1980.

About the Author

KENNETH NAVERSEN is a photographer and writer who specializes in architectural and travel subjects. He has a masters degree in art history and photography and is a former recipient of an Art Critics Fellowship Grant from the National Endowment for the Arts. His photographic work has appeared in numerous regional and national publications. His writing credits include three previous books on vintage architecture, the most recent of which, *California Victorians,* was published by Beautiful America Publishing Company in 1998.

Patrick Clark Mansion, Spokane, 1898